THE DUMP FILES

The Dump Files

Please Seat Yourself

Date

___ - ___ - ___

Name

_____

Favorite Song At The Moment

Song _____

Artist _____

Favorite Movie At The Moment

_____

URGENCY

WATCH OUT!
NORMAL
LOW
SHADE

Time In   Time Out

_____ A / P   _____ A / P

What Brings You Here?

#1 _____   #2 _____   #3 _____

Words Of Encouragement

_____
_____
_____
_____

Plans For The Day

_____
_____
_____
_____

Did You Search The Web?

Yes ○   No ○

If So, For... _____
_____

Your Favorite Name For This Room

Bathroom	○	The Crapper	○
The Throne	○	The Shitter	○
The Can	○	The Pot	○
Powder Room	○	The Loo	○
The Jon	○	Other: _____	

ROOM RATINGS:

	1	2	3	4	5
CLEAN	○	○	○	○	○
COMFORTABLE	○	○	○	○	○
READING MATERIALS	○	○	○	○	○
ROOMY	○	○	○	○	○
T P	○	○	○	○	○
FLUSH	○	○	○	○	○
SPRAY	○	○	○	○	○
OVERALL	○	○	○	○	○

The Dump Files

Please Seat Yourself

Date

- - - _____

Favorite Song At The Moment

Song _____

Artist _____

Favorite Movie At The Moment

_____

.

URGENCY

WATCH OUT!
NORMAL
LOW
SHADE

Name

_____

Time In   Time Out

_____ A / P   _____ A / P

What Brings You Here?

#1 _____   #2 _____   #3 _____

Words Of Encouragement

_____

_____

_____

_____

_____

Plans For The Day

_____

_____

_____

_____

Did You Search The Web?

Yes ○   No ○

If So, For... _____

_____

Your Favorite Name For This Room

Bathroom	○	The Crapper	○
The Throne	○	The Shitter	○
The Can	○	The Pot	○
Powder Room	○	The Loo	○
The Jon	○	Other: _____	

ROOM RATINGS:

	1	2	3	4	5
CLEAN	○	○	○	○	○
COMFORTABLE	○	○	○	○	○
READING MATERIALS	○	○	○	○	○
ROOMY	○	○	○	○	○
T P	○	○	○	○	○
FLUSH	○	○	○	○	○
SPRAY	○	○	○	○	○
OVERALL	○	○	○	○	○

The Dump Files

Please Seat Yourself

Date
- -
_____

Name
_____

Did You Search The Web?
Yes ○   No ○

If So, For... _____
_____

Favorite Song At The Moment

Song _____

Artist _____

Time In   Time Out
_____ A / P   _____ A / P

What Brings You Here?
#1 _____   #2 _____   #3 _____

Your Favorite Name For This Room

Bathroom	○	The Crapper	○
The Throne	○	The Shitter	○
The Can	○	The Pot	○
Powder Room	○	The Loo	○
The Jon	○	Other: _____	

Favorite Movie At The Moment
_____

Words Of Encouragement
_____
_____
_____
_____

ROOM RATINGS:

	1	2	3	4	5
CLEAN	○	○	○	○	○
COMFORTABLE	○	○	○	○	○
READING MATERIALS	○	○	○	○	○
ROOMY	○	○	○	○	○
T P	○	○	○	○	○
FLUSH	○	○	○	○	○
SPRAY	○	○	○	○	○
OVERALL	○	○	○	○	○

URGENCY

WATCH OUT!
NORMAL
LOW
SHADE

Plans For The Day
_____
_____
_____

The Dump Files

Please Seat Yourself

Date

__ - __ -

_____

Favorite Song At The Moment

Song _____

Artist _____

Favorite Movie At The Moment

_____

URGENCY

WATCH OUT!
NORMAL
LOW
SHADE

Name

_____

Time In	Time Out
_____ A / P	_____ A / P

What Brings You Here?

#1 _____   #2 _____   #3 _____

Words Of Encouragement

_____

_____

_____

_____

Plans For The Day

_____

_____

_____

_____

Did You Search The Web?

Yes ○   No ○

If So, For... _____

_____

Your Favorite Name For This Room

Bathroom	○	The Crapper	○
The Throne	○	The Shitter	○
The Can	○	The Pot	○
Powder Room	○	The Loo	○
The Jon	○	Other: _____	

ROOM RATINGS:

	1	2	3	4	5
CLEAN	○	○	○	○	○
COMFORTABLE	○	○	○	○	○
READING MATERIALS	○	○	○	○	○
ROOMY	○	○	○	○	○
T P	○	○	○	○	○
FLUSH	○	○	○	○	○
SPRAY	○	○	○	○	○
OVERALL	○	○	○	○	○

The Dump Files

Please Seat Yourself

Date
___ - ___ - ___

Name
_____

Did You Search The Web?
Yes ○   No ○

If So, For... _____
_____

Favorite Song At The Moment

Song _____

Artist _____

Time In   Time Out
_____ A / P   _____ A / P

What Brings You Here?
#1 _____ #2 _____ #3 _____

Your Favorite Name For This Room

Bathroom	○	The Crapper	○
The Throne	○	The Shitter	○
The Can	○	The Pot	○
Powder Room	○	The Loo	○
The Jon	○	Other: _____	

Favorite Movie At The Moment

_____

Words Of Encouragement

_____
_____
_____
_____
_____

URGENCY

WATCH OUT!
NORMAL
LOW
SHADE

Plans For The Day

_____
_____
_____
_____

ROOM RATINGS:

	1	2	3	4	5
CLEAN	○	○	○	○	○
COMFORTABLE	○	○	○	○	○
READING MATERIALS	○	○	○	○	○
ROOMY	○	○	○	○	○
T P	○	○	○	○	○
FLUSH	○	○	○	○	○
SPRAY	○	○	○	○	○
OVERALL	○	○	○	○	○

The Dump Files

Please Seat Yourself

Date

_ - _ - _____

Name

_____

Favorite Song At The Moment

Song _____

Artist _____

Favorite Movie At The Moment

_____

URGENCY

| WATCH OUT! |
| NORMAL |
| LOW |
| SHADE |

Time In   Time Out

_____ A / P   _____ A / P

What Brings You Here?

#1 _____   #2 _____   #3 _____

Words Of Encouragement

_____

_____

_____

_____

Plans For The Day

_____

_____

_____

_____

Did You Search The Web?

Yes ○   No ○

If So, For... _____

_____

Your Favorite Name For This Room

Bathroom	○	The Crapper	○
The Throne	○	The Shitter	○
The Can	○	The Pot	○
Powder Room	○	The Loo	○
The Jon	○	Other: _____	

ROOM RATINGS:

	1	2	3	4	5
CLEAN	○	○	○	○	○
COMFORTABLE	○	○	○	○	○
READING MATERIALS	○	○	○	○	○
ROOMY	○	○	○	○	○
T P	○	○	○	○	○
FLUSH	○	○	○	○	○
SPRAY	○	○	○	○	○
OVERALL	○	○	○	○	○

The Dump Files

Please Seat Yourself

Date

_____ - _____ - _____

Name

_____

Favorite Song At The Moment

Song _____

Artist _____

Time In   Time Out

_____ A / P   _____ A / P

What Brings You Here?

#1 _____   #2 _____   #3 _____

Favorite Movie At The Moment

_____

Words Of Encouragement

_____

_____

_____

_____

URGENCY

| WATCH OUT! |
| NORMAL |
| LOW |
| SHADE |

Plans For The Day

_____

_____

_____

Did You Search The Web?

Yes ○   No ○

If So, For... _____

_____

Your Favorite Name For This Room

Bathroom	○	The Crapper	○
The Throne	○	The Shitter	○
The Can	○	The Pot	○
Powder Room	○	The Loo	○
The Jon	○	Other: _____	

ROOM RATINGS:

	1	2	3	4	5
CLEAN	○	○	○	○	○
COMFORTABLE	○	○	○	○	○
READING MATERIALS	○	○	○	○	○
ROOMY	○	○	○	○	○
T P	○	○	○	○	○
FLUSH	○	○	○	○	○
SPRAY	○	○	○	○	○
OVERALL	○	○	○	○	○

The Dump Files

Please Seat Yourself

Date

___ - ___ - ___

Name

_____

Did You Search The Web?

Yes ○   No ○

If So, For... _____

_____

Favorite Song At The Moment

Song _____

Artist _____

Time In   Time Out

_____ A / P   _____ A / P

What Brings You Here?

#1 _____ #2 _____ #3 _____

Your Favorite Name For This Room

Bathroom	○	The Crapper	○
The Throne	○	The Shitter	○
The Can	○	The Pot	○
Powder Room	○	The Loo	○
The Jon	○	Other: _____	

Favorite Movie At The Moment

_____

Words Of Encouragement

_____

_____

_____

_____

URGENCY

WATCH OUT!
NORMAL
LOW
SHADE

Plans For The Day

_____

_____

_____

_____

ROOM RATINGS:

	1	2	3	4	5
CLEAN	○	○	○	○	○
COMFORTABLE	○	○	○	○	○
READING MATERIALS	○	○	○	○	○
ROOMY	○	○	○	○	○
T P	○	○	○	○	○
FLUSH	○	○	○	○	○
SPRAY	○	○	○	○	○
OVERALL	○	○	○	○	○

The Dump Files

Please Seat Yourself

Date

_ _

_____

Name

_____

Did You Search The Web?

Yes ○   No ○

If So, For... _____

_____

Favorite Song At The Moment

Song _____

Artist _____

Time In   Time Out

_____ A / P   _____ A / P

What Brings You Here?

#1 _____ #2 _____ #3 _____

Your Favorite Name For This Room

Bathroom	○	The Crapper	○
The Throne	○	The Shitter	○
The Can	○	The Pot	○
Powder Room	○	The Loo	○
The Jon	○	Other: _____	

Favorite Movie At The Moment

_____

Words Of Encouragement

_____

_____

_____

_____

URGENCY

WATCH OUT!
NORMAL
LOW
SHADE

Plans For The Day

_____

_____

_____

ROOM RATINGS:

	1	2	3	4	5
CLEAN	○	○	○	○	○
COMFORTABLE	○	○	○	○	○
READING MATERIALS	○	○	○	○	○
ROOMY	○	○	○	○	○
T P	○	○	○	○	○
FLUSH	○	○	○	○	○
SPRAY	○	○	○	○	○
OVERALL	○	○	○	○	○

The Dump Files

Please Seat Yourself

Date
___ - ___ - ___

Name
_____

Favorite Song At The Moment
Song _____

Artist _____

Time In   Time Out
_____ A / P   _____ A / P

What Brings You Here?
#1 _____   #2 _____   #3 _____

Your Favorite Name For This Room
Bathroom ○   The Crapper ○
The Throne ○   The Shitter ○
The Can ○   The Pot ○
Powder Room ○   The Loo ○
The Jon ○   Other: _____

Favorite Movie At The Moment
_____

Words Of Encouragement
_____
_____
_____
_____

ROOM RATINGS:

	1	2	3	4	5
CLEAN	○	○	○	○	○
COMFORTABLE	○	○	○	○	○
READING MATERIALS	○	○	○	○	○
ROOMY	○	○	○	○	○
T P	○	○	○	○	○
FLUSH	○	○	○	○	○
SPRAY	○	○	○	○	○
OVERALL	○	○	○	○	○

URGENCY

| WATCH OUT! |
| NORMAL |
| LOW |
| SHADE |

Plans For The Day
_____
_____
_____

The Dump Files

Please Seat Yourself

Date
_____ - _____ - _____

Name
_____

Did You Search The Web?
Yes ○   No ○

If So, For... _____

_____

Favorite Song At The Moment

Song _____

Artist _____

Time In   Time Out
_____ A / P   _____ A / P

What Brings You Here?
#1 _____   #2 _____   #3 _____

Your Favorite Name For This Room

Bathroom	○	The Crapper	○
The Throne	○	The Shitter	○
The Can	○	The Pot	○
Powder Room	○	The Loo	○
The Jon	○	Other: _____	

Favorite Movie At The Moment
_____

Words Of Encouragement
_____

_____

_____

_____

URGENCY

WATCH OUT!
NORMAL
LOW
SHADE

Plans For The Day
_____

_____

_____

ROOM RATINGS:

	1	2	3	4	5
CLEAN	○	○	○	○	○
COMFORTABLE	○	○	○	○	○
READING MATERIALS	○	○	○	○	○
ROOMY	○	○	○	○	○
T P	○	○	○	○	○
FLUSH	○	○	○	○	○
SPRAY	○	○	○	○	○
OVERALL	○	○	○	○	○

The Dump Files

Please Seat Yourself

Date

___ - ___ - ___

Name

_____

Did You Search The Web?

Yes ○   No ○

If So, For... _____

_____

Favorite Song At The Moment

Song _____

Artist _____

Time In   Time Out

_____ A / P   _____ A / P

What Brings You Here?

#1 _____ #2 _____ #3 _____

Your Favorite Name For This Room

Bathroom	○	The Crapper	○
The Throne	○	The Shitter	○
The Can	○	The Pot	○
Powder Room	○	The Loo	○
The Jon	○	Other: _____	

Favorite Movie At The Moment

_____

Words Of Encouragement

_____

_____

_____

_____

URGENCY

WATCH OUT!
NORMAL
LOW
SHADE

Plans For The Day

_____

_____

_____

_____

ROOM RATINGS:

	1	2	3	4	5
CLEAN	○	○	○	○	○
COMFORTABLE	○	○	○	○	○
READING MATERIALS	○	○	○	○	○
ROOMY	○	○	○	○	○
T P	○	○	○	○	○
FLUSH	○	○	○	○	○
SPRAY	○	○	○	○	○
OVERALL	○	○	○	○	○

The Dump Files

Please Seat Yourself

Date

___ - ___ - ___

Name

_____

Favorite Song At The Moment

Song _____

Artist _____

Time In   Time Out

_____ A / P   _____ A / P

What Brings You Here?

#1 _____   #2 _____   #3 _____

Your Favorite Name For This Room

Bathroom	○	The Crapper	○
The Throne	○	The Shitter	○
The Can	○	The Pot	○
Powder Room	○	The Loo	○
The Jon	○	Other: _____	

Favorite Movie At The Moment

_____

Words Of Encouragement

_____
_____
_____
_____
_____

URGENCY

| WATCH OUT! |
| NORMAL |
| LOW |
| SHADE |

Plans For The Day

_____
_____
_____
_____

ROOM RATINGS:

	1	2	3	4	5
CLEAN	○	○	○	○	○
COMFORTABLE	○	○	○	○	○
READING MATERIALS	○	○	○	○	○
ROOMY	○	○	○	○	○
T P	○	○	○	○	○
FLUSH	○	○	○	○	○
SPRAY	○	○	○	○	○
OVERALL	○	○	○	○	○

The Dump Files

Please Seat Yourself

Date

____ - ____ - ____

Name

_____

Did You Search The Web?

Yes ○   No ○

If So, For... _____

_____

Favorite Song At The Moment

Song _____

Artist _____

Time In   Time Out

_____ A / P   _____ A / P

What Brings You Here?

#1 _____   #2 _____   #3 _____

Your Favorite Name For This Room

Bathroom	○	The Crapper	○
The Throne	○	The Shitter	○
The Can	○	The Pot	○
Powder Room	○	The Loo	○
The Jon	○	Other: _____	

Favorite Movie At The Moment

_____

Words Of Encouragement

_____

_____

_____

_____

ROOM RATINGS:

	1	2	3	4	5
CLEAN	○	○	○	○	○
COMFORTABLE	○	○	○	○	○
READING MATERIALS	○	○	○	○	○
ROOMY	○	○	○	○	○
T P	○	○	○	○	○
FLUSH	○	○	○	○	○
SPRAY	○	○	○	○	○
OVERALL	○	○	○	○	○

URGENCY

WATCH OUT!
NORMAL
LOW
SHADE

Plans For The Day

_____

_____

_____

The Dump Files

Please Seat Yourself

Date

__ - __ - __

_____

Favorite Song At The Moment

Song _____

Artist _____

Favorite Movie At The Moment

_____

URGENCY

| WATCH OUT! |
| NORMAL |
| LOW |
| SHADE |

Name

_____

Time In   Time Out

_____ A / P   _____ A / P

What Brings You Here?

#1 _____   #2 _____   #3 _____

Words Of Encouragement

_____
_____
_____
_____

Plans For The Day

_____
_____
_____
_____

Did You Search The Web?

Yes ○   No ○

If So, For... _____

_____

Your Favorite Name For This Room

Bathroom	○	The Crapper	○
The Throne	○	The Shitter	○
The Can	○	The Pot	○
Powder Room	○	The Loo	○
The Jon	○	Other: _____	

ROOM RATINGS:

	1	2	3	4	5
CLEAN	○	○	○	○	○
COMFORTABLE	○	○	○	○	○
READING MATERIALS	○	○	○	○	○
ROOMY	○	○	○	○	○
T P	○	○	○	○	○
FLUSH	○	○	○	○	○
SPRAY	○	○	○	○	○
OVERALL	○	○	○	○	○

The Dump Files

Please Seat Yourself

Date

___ - ___ - _____

Favorite Song At The Moment

Song _____

Artist _____

Favorite Movie At The Moment

_____

URGENCY

WATCH OUT!
NORMAL
LOW
SHADE

Name

_____

Time In	Time Out
_____ A / P	_____ A / P

What Brings You Here?

#1 _____ #2 _____ #3 _____

Words Of Encouragement

_____

_____

_____

_____

Plans For The Day

_____

_____

_____

_____

Did You Search The Web?

Yes ○   No ○

If So, For... _____

_____

Your Favorite Name For This Room

Bathroom	○	The Crapper	○
The Throne	○	The Shitter	○
The Can	○	The Pot	○
Powder Room	○	The Loo	○
The Jon	○	Other: _____	

ROOM RATINGS:

	1	2	3	4	5
CLEAN	○	○	○	○	○
COMFORTABLE	○	○	○	○	○
READING MATERIALS	○	○	○	○	○
ROOMY	○	○	○	○	○
T P	○	○	○	○	○
FLUSH	○	○	○	○	○
SPRAY	○	○	○	○	○
OVERALL	○	○	○	○	○

The Dump Files

Please Seat Yourself

Date

___ - ___ - ___

Name

_____

Favorite Song At The Moment

Song _____

Artist _____

Favorite Movie At The Moment

_____

URGENCY

WATCH OUT!
NORMAL
LOW
SHADE

Time In _____ A / P   Time Out _____ A / P

What Brings You Here?

#1 _____   #2 _____   #3 _____

Words Of Encouragement

_____
_____
_____
_____

Plans For The Day

_____
_____
_____
_____

Did You Search The Web?

Yes ○   No ○

If So, For... _____
_____

Your Favorite Name For This Room

Bathroom	○	The Crapper	○
The Throne	○	The Shitter	○
The Can	○	The Pot	○
Powder Room	○	The Loo	○
The Jon	○	Other: _____	

ROOM RATINGS:

	1	2	3	4	5
CLEAN	○	○	○	○	○
COMFORTABLE	○	○	○	○	○
READING MATERIALS	○	○	○	○	○
ROOMY	○	○	○	○	○
T P	○	○	○	○	○
FLUSH	○	○	○	○	○
SPRAY	○	○	○	○	○
OVERALL	○	○	○	○	○

The Dump Files

Please Seat Yourself

Date

___ - ___ - _____

Favorite Song At The Moment

Song _____

Artist _____

Favorite Movie At The Moment

_____

URGENCY

| WATCH OUT! |
| NORMAL |
| LOW |
| SHADE |

Name

_____

Time In	Time Out
_____ A / P	_____ A / P

What Brings You Here?

#1 _____ #2 _____ #3 _____

Words Of Encouragement

_____

_____

_____

_____

Plans For The Day

_____

_____

_____

_____

Did You Search The Web?

Yes ○   No ○

If So, For... _____

_____

Your Favorite Name For This Room

Bathroom	○	The Crapper	○
The Throne	○	The Shitter	○
The Can	○	The Pot	○
Powder Room	○	The Loo	○
The Jon	○	Other: _____	

ROOM RATINGS:

	1	2	3	4	5
CLEAN	○	○	○	○	○
COMFORTABLE	○	○	○	○	○
READING MATERIALS	○	○	○	○	○
ROOMY	○	○	○	○	○
T P	○	○	○	○	○
FLUSH	○	○	○	○	○
SPRAY	○	○	○	○	○
OVERALL	○	○	○	○	○

The Dump Files

Please Seat Yourself

Date
_ _ _ - _ _ _ - _ _ _

Name
_____

Did You Search The Web?
Yes ○   No ○

If So, For... _____

_____

Favorite Song At The Moment

Song _____

Artist _____

Time In   Time Out
_____ A / P   _____ A / P

What Brings You Here?
#1 _____   #2 _____   #3 _____

Your Favorite Name For This Room

Bathroom	○	The Crapper	○
The Throne	○	The Shitter	○
The Can	○	The Pot	○
Powder Room	○	The Loo	○
The Jon	○	Other: _____	

Favorite Movie At The Moment

_____

Words Of Encouragement

_____

_____

_____

_____

ROOM RATINGS:

	1	2	3	4	5
CLEAN	○	○	○	○	○
COMFORTABLE	○	○	○	○	○
READING MATERIALS	○	○	○	○	○
ROOMY	○	○	○	○	○
T P	○	○	○	○	○
FLUSH	○	○	○	○	○
SPRAY	○	○	○	○	○
OVERALL	○	○	○	○	○

URGENCY

WATCH OUT!
NORMAL
LOW
SHADE

Plans For The Day

_____

_____

_____

_____

The Dump Files

Please Seat Yourself

Date

- - -

_____

Favorite Song At The Moment

Song _____

Artist _____

Favorite Movie At The Moment

_____

URGENCY

WATCH OUT!
NORMAL
LOW
SHADE

Name

_____

Time In	Time Out
_____ A / P	_____ A / P

What Brings You Here?

#1 _____ #2 _____ #3 _____

Words Of Encouragement

_____
_____
_____
_____
_____

Plans For The Day

_____
_____
_____
_____

Did You Search The Web?

Yes ○   No ○

If So, For... _____
_____

Your Favorite Name For This Room

Bathroom	○	The Crapper	○
The Throne	○	The Shitter	○
The Can	○	The Pot	○
Powder Room	○	The Loo	○
The Jon	○	Other: _____	

ROOM RATINGS:

	1	2	3	4	5
CLEAN	○	○	○	○	○
COMFORTABLE	○	○	○	○	○
READING MATERIALS	○	○	○	○	○
ROOMY	○	○	○	○	○
T P	○	○	○	○	○
FLUSH	○	○	○	○	○
SPRAY	○	○	○	○	○
OVERALL	○	○	○	○	○

The Dump Files

Please Seat Yourself

Date

_____ - _____ - _____

Name

_____

Favorite Song At The Moment

Song _____

Artist _____

Time In   Time Out

_____ A / P   _____ A / P

What Brings You Here?

#1 _____   #2 _____   #3 _____

Your Favorite Name For This Room

Bathroom	○	The Crapper	○
The Throne	○	The Shitter	○
The Can	○	The Pot	○
Powder Room	○	The Loo	○
The Jon	○	Other: _____	

Favorite Movie At The Moment

_____

Words Of Encouragement

_____
_____
_____
_____
_____

URGENCY

WATCH OUT!
NORMAL
LOW
SHADE

Plans For The Day

_____
_____
_____
_____

ROOM RATINGS:

	1	2	3	4	5
CLEAN	○	○	○	○	○
COMFORTABLE	○	○	○	○	○
READING MATERIALS	○	○	○	○	○
ROOMY	○	○	○	○	○
T P	○	○	○	○	○
FLUSH	○	○	○	○	○
SPRAY	○	○	○	○	○
OVERALL	○	○	○	○	○

The Dump Files

Please Seat Yourself

Date

___ - ___ - ___

Name

_____

Did You Search The Web?

Yes ○   No ○

If So, For... _____
_____

Favorite Song At The Moment

Song _____

Artist _____

Time In   Time Out

_____ A / P   _____ A / P

What Brings You Here?

#1 _____ #2 _____ #3 _____

Your Favorite Name For This Room

Bathroom	○	The Crapper	○
The Throne	○	The Shitter	○
The Can	○	The Pot	○
Powder Room	○	The Loo	○
The Jon	○	Other: _____	

Favorite Movie At The Moment

_____

Words Of Encouragement

_____
_____
_____
_____

ROOM RATINGS:

	1	2	3	4	5
CLEAN	○	○	○	○	○
COMFORTABLE	○	○	○	○	○
READING MATERIALS	○	○	○	○	○
ROOMY	○	○	○	○	○
T P	○	○	○	○	○
FLUSH	○	○	○	○	○
SPRAY	○	○	○	○	○
OVERALL	○	○	○	○	○

URGENCY

WATCH OUT!
NORMAL
LOW
SHADE

Plans For The Day

_____
_____
_____
_____

The Dump Files
Please Seat Yourself

Date
___ - ___ - ___

Favorite Song At The Moment
Song _____

Artist _____

Favorite Movie At The Moment
_____

URGENCY

WATCH OUT!
NORMAL
LOW
SHADE

Name
_____

Time In   Time Out
_____ A / P   _____ A / P

What Brings You Here?
#1 _____ #2 _____ #3 _____

Words Of Encouragement
_____
_____
_____
_____

Plans For The Day
_____
_____
_____

Did You Search The Web?
Yes ○   No ○

If So, For... _____
_____

Your Favorite Name For This Room
Bathroom	○	The Crapper	○
The Throne	○	The Shitter	○
The Can	○	The Pot	○
Powder Room	○	The Loo	○
The Jon	○	Other: _____	

ROOM RATINGS:
	1	2	3	4	5
CLEAN	○	○	○	○	○
COMFORTABLE	○	○	○	○	○
READING MATERIALS	○	○	○	○	○
ROOMY	○	○	○	○	○
T P	○	○	○	○	○
FLUSH	○	○	○	○	○
SPRAY	○	○	○	○	○
OVERALL	○	○	○	○	○

The Dump Files

Please Seat Yourself

Date

___ - ___ - ___

Favorite Song At The Moment

Song _____

Artist _____

Favorite Movie At The Moment

_____

URGENCY

| WATCH OUT! |
| NORMAL |
| LOW |
| SHADE |

Name

_____

Time In	Time Out
_____ A / P	_____ A / P

What Brings You Here?

#1 _____   #2 _____   #3 _____

Words Of Encouragement

_____
_____
_____
_____

Plans For The Day

_____
_____
_____
_____

Did You Search The Web?

Yes ○   No ○

If So, For... _____
_____

Your Favorite Name For This Room

Bathroom	○	The Crapper	○
The Throne	○	The Shitter	○
The Can	○	The Pot	○
Powder Room	○	The Loo	○
The Jon	○	Other: _____

ROOM RATINGS:

	1	2	3	4	5
CLEAN	○	○	○	○	○
COMFORTABLE	○	○	○	○	○
READING MATERIALS	○	○	○	○	○
ROOMY	○	○	○	○	○
T P	○	○	○	○	○
FLUSH	○	○	○	○	○
SPRAY	○	○	○	○	○
OVERALL	○	○	○	○	○

The Dump Files
Please Seat Yourself

Date
___-___-___

Name
_____

Favorite Song At The Moment
Song _____
Artist _____

Time In   **Time Out**
_____ A / P   _____ A / P

What Brings You Here?
#1 _____ #2 _____ #3 _____

Your Favorite Name For This Room

Bathroom	○	The Crapper	○
The Throne	○	The Shitter	○
The Can	○	The Pot	○
Powder Room	○	The Loo	○
The Jon	○	Other: _____	

Favorite Movie At The Moment
_____

Words Of Encouragement
_____
_____
_____
_____

URGENCY

WATCH OUT!
NORMAL
LOW
SHADE

Plans For The Day
_____
_____
_____
_____

ROOM RATINGS:

	1	2	3	4	5
CLEAN	○	○	○	○	○
COMFORTABLE	○	○	○	○	○
READING MATERIALS	○	○	○	○	○
ROOMY	○	○	○	○	○
T P	○	○	○	○	○
FLUSH	○	○	○	○	○
SPRAY	○	○	○	○	○
OVERALL	○	○	○	○	○

The Dump Files

Please Seat Yourself

Date

___ - ___ - ___

Favorite Song At The Moment

Song _____

Artist _____

Favorite Movie At The Moment

_____

URGENCY

WATCH OUT!
NORMAL
LOW
SHADE

Name

_____

Time In   Time Out

_____ A / P   _____ A / P

What Brings You Here?

#1 _____   #2 _____   #3 _____

Words Of Encouragement

_____

_____

_____

_____

Plans For The Day

_____

_____

_____

_____

Did You Search The Web?

Yes ○   No ○

If So, For... _____

_____

Your Favorite Name For This Room

Bathroom	○	The Crapper	○
The Throne	○	The Shitter	○
The Can	○	The Pot	○
Powder Room	○	The Loo	○
The Jon	○	Other: _____	

ROOM RATINGS:

	1	2	3	4	5
CLEAN	○	○	○	○	○
COMFORTABLE	○	○	○	○	○
READING MATERIALS	○	○	○	○	○
ROOMY	○	○	○	○	○
T P	○	○	○	○	○
FLUSH	○	○	○	○	○
SPRAY	○	○	○	○	○
OVERALL	○	○	○	○	○

The Dump Files

Please Seat Yourself

Date
_____-_____-_____

Favorite Song At The Moment
Song _____

Artist _____

Favorite Movie At The Moment
_____

URGENCY

WATCH OUT!
NORMAL
LOW
SHADE

Name
_____

Time In	Time Out
_____ A / P	_____ A / P

What Brings You Here?
#1 _____ #2 _____ #3 _____

Words Of Encouragement
_____

_____

_____

_____

Plans For The Day
_____

_____

_____

Did You Search The Web?
Yes ○   No ○

If So, For... _____

_____

Your Favorite Name For This Room

Bathroom	○	The Crapper	○
The Throne	○	The Shitter	○
The Can	○	The Pot	○
Powder Room	○	The Loo	○
The Jon	○	Other: _____	

ROOM RATINGS:

	1	2	3	4	5
CLEAN	○	○	○	○	○
COMFORTABLE	○	○	○	○	○
READING MATERIALS	○	○	○	○	○
ROOMY	○	○	○	○	○
T P	○	○	○	○	○
FLUSH	○	○	○	○	○
SPRAY	○	○	○	○	○
OVERALL	○	○	○	○	○

The Dump Files

Please Seat Yourself

Date

___ - ___ - ___

Favorite Song At The Moment

Song _____

Artist _____

Favorite Movie At The Moment

_____

URGENCY

WATCH OUT!
NORMAL
LOW
SHADE

Name

_____

Time In   Time Out

_____ A / P   _____ A / P

What Brings You Here?

#1 _____   #2 _____   #3 _____

Words Of Encouragement

_____

_____

_____

_____

_____

Plans For The Day

_____

_____

_____

_____

Did You Search The Web?

Yes ○   No ○

If So, For... _____

_____

Your Favorite Name For This Room

Bathroom	○	The Crapper	○
The Throne	○	The Shitter	○
The Can	○	The Pot	○
Powder Room	○	The Loo	○
The Jon	○	Other: _____	

ROOM RATINGS:

	1	2	3	4	5
CLEAN	○	○	○	○	○
COMFORTABLE	○	○	○	○	○
READING MATERIALS	○	○	○	○	○
ROOMY	○	○	○	○	○
T P	○	○	○	○	○
FLUSH	○	○	○	○	○
SPRAY	○	○	○	○	○
OVERALL	○	○	○	○	○

The Dump Files

Please Seat Yourself

Date

____ - ____ - ____

Favorite Song At The Moment

Song _____

Artist _____

Favorite Movie At The Moment

_____

URGENCY

| WATCH OUT! |
| NORMAL |
| LOW |
| SHADE |

Name

_____

Time In	Time Out
_____ A / P	_____ A / P

What Brings You Here?

#1 _____ #2 _____ #3 _____

Words Of Encouragement

_____
_____
_____
_____

Plans For The Day

_____
_____
_____

Did You Search The Web?

Yes ○   No ○

If So, For... _____

_____

Your Favorite Name For This Room

Bathroom ○	The Crapper ○
The Throne ○	The Shitter ○
The Can ○	The Pot ○
Powder Room ○	The Loo ○
The Jon ○	Other: _____

ROOM RATINGS:

	1	2	3	4	5
CLEAN	○	○	○	○	○
COMFORTABLE	○	○	○	○	○
READING MATERIALS	○	○	○	○	○
ROOMY	○	○	○	○	○
T P	○	○	○	○	○
FLUSH	○	○	○	○	○
SPRAY	○	○	○	○	○
OVERALL	○	○	○	○	○

The Dump Files

Please Seat Yourself

Date
_____ - _____ - _____

Name
_____

Did You Search The Web?
Yes ○   No ○

If So, For... _____
_____

Favorite Song At The Moment

Song _____

Artist _____

Time In   Time Out
_____ A / P   _____ A / P

What Brings You Here?
#1 _____   #2 _____   #3 _____

Your Favorite Name For This Room

Bathroom	○	The Crapper	○
The Throne	○	The Shitter	○
The Can	○	The Pot	○
Powder Room	○	The Loo	○
The Jon	○	Other: _____	

Favorite Movie At The Moment
_____

Words Of Encouragement
_____
_____
_____
_____

URGENCY

WATCH OUT!
NORMAL
LOW
SHADE

Plans For The Day
_____
_____
_____

ROOM RATINGS:

	1	2	3	4	5
CLEAN	○	○	○	○	○
COMFORTABLE	○	○	○	○	○
READING MATERIALS	○	○	○	○	○
ROOMY	○	○	○	○	○
T P	○	○	○	○	○
FLUSH	○	○	○	○	○
SPRAY	○	○	○	○	○
OVERALL	○	○	○	○	○

The Dump Files

Please Seat Yourself

Date

___ - ___ - ___

Name

_____

Did You Search The Web?

Yes ○   No ○

If So, For... _____

_____

Favorite Song At The Moment

Song _____

Artist _____

Time In   Time Out

_____ A / P   _____ A / P

What Brings You Here?

#1 _____   #2 _____   #3 _____

Your Favorite Name For This Room

Bathroom	○	The Crapper	○
The Throne	○	The Shitter	○
The Can	○	The Pot	○
Powder Room	○	The Loo	○
The Jon	○	Other: _____	

Favorite Movie At The Moment

_____

Words Of Encouragement

_____
_____
_____
_____

URGENCY

WATCH OUT!
NORMAL
LOW
SHADE

Plans For The Day

_____
_____
_____

ROOM RATINGS:

	1	2	3	4	5
CLEAN	○	○	○	○	○
COMFORTABLE	○	○	○	○	○
READING MATERIALS	○	○	○	○	○
ROOMY	○	○	○	○	○
T P	○	○	○	○	○
FLUSH	○	○	○	○	○
SPRAY	○	○	○	○	○
OVERALL	○	○	○	○	○

The Dump Files

Please Seat Yourself

Date

_ - _ -_
_____

Favorite Song At The Moment

Song _____

Artist _____

Favorite Movie At The Moment

_____

URGENCY

| WATCH OUT! |
| NORMAL |
| LOW |
| SHADE |

Name

_____

Time In	Time Out
_____ A / P	_____ A / P

What Brings You Here?

#1 _____   #2 _____   #3 _____

Words Of Encouragement

_____
_____
_____
_____

Plans For The Day

_____
_____
_____
_____

Did You Search The Web?

Yes ○   No ○

If So, For... _____
_____

Your Favorite Name For This Room

Bathroom	○	The Crapper	○
The Throne	○	The Shitter	○
The Can	○	The Pot	○
Powder Room	○	The Loo	○
The Jon	○	Other: _____	

ROOM RATINGS:

	1	2	3	4	5
CLEAN	○	○	○	○	○
COMFORTABLE	○	○	○	○	○
READING MATERIALS	○	○	○	○	○
ROOMY	○	○	○	○	○
T P	○	○	○	○	○
FLUSH	○	○	○	○	○
SPRAY	○	○	○	○	○
OVERALL	○	○	○	○	○

The Dump Files

Please Seat Yourself

Date

___ - ___ - ___

Favorite Song At The Moment

Song _____

Artist _____

Favorite Movie At The Moment

_____

URGENCY

WATCH OUT!
NORMAL
LOW
SHADE

Name

_____

Time In   Time Out

_____ A / P   _____ A / P

What Brings You Here?

#1 _____   #2 _____   #3 _____

Words Of Encouragement

_____
_____
_____
_____

Plans For The Day

_____
_____
_____
_____

Did You Search The Web?

Yes ○   No ○

If So, For... _____
_____

Your Favorite Name For This Room

Bathroom	○	The Crapper	○
The Throne	○	The Shitter	○
The Can	○	The Pot	○
Powder Room	○	The Loo	○
The Jon	○	Other: _____	

ROOM RATINGS:

	1	2	3	4	5
CLEAN	○	○	○	○	○
COMFORTABLE	○	○	○	○	○
READING MATERIALS	○	○	○	○	○
ROOMY	○	○	○	○	○
T P	○	○	○	○	○
FLUSH	○	○	○	○	○
SPRAY	○	○	○	○	○
OVERALL	○	○	○	○	○

The Dump Files

Please Seat Yourself

Date

- - -

Favorite Song At The Moment

Song _____

Artist _____

Favorite Movie At The Moment

_____

URGENCY

WATCH OUT!
NORMAL
LOW
SHADE

Name

_____

Time In   Time Out

_____ A / P   _____ A / P

What Brings You Here?

#1 _____   #2 _____   #3 _____

Words Of Encouragement

_____

_____

_____

_____

Plans For The Day

_____

_____

_____

_____

Did You Search The Web?

Yes ○   No ○

If So, For... _____

_____

Your Favorite Name For This Room

Bathroom	○	The Crapper	○
The Throne	○	The Shitter	○
The Can	○	The Pot	○
Powder Room	○	The Loo	○
The Jon	○	Other: _____	

ROOM RATINGS:

	1	2	3	4	5
CLEAN	○	○	○	○	○
COMFORTABLE	○	○	○	○	○
READING MATERIALS	○	○	○	○	○
ROOMY	○	○	○	○	○
T P	○	○	○	○	○
FLUSH	○	○	○	○	○
SPRAY	○	○	○	○	○
OVERALL	○	○	○	○	○

The Dump Files

Please Seat Yourself

Date

_____-_____-_____

Favorite Song At The Moment

Song _____

Artist _____

Favorite Movie At The Moment

_____

URGENCY

WATCH OUT!
NORMAL
LOW
SHADE

Name

_____

Time In   Time Out

_____ A / P   _____ A / P

What Brings You Here?

#1 _____   #2 _____   #3 _____

Words Of Encouragement

_____
_____
_____
_____

Plans For The Day

_____
_____
_____
_____

Did You Search The Web?

Yes ○   No ○

If So, For... _____

_____

Your Favorite Name For This Room

Bathroom	○	The Crapper	○
The Throne	○	The Shitter	○
The Can	○	The Pot	○
Powder Room	○	The Loo	○
The Jon	○	Other: _____	

ROOM RATINGS:

	1	2	3	4	5
CLEAN	○	○	○	○	○
COMFORTABLE	○	○	○	○	○
READING MATERIALS	○	○	○	○	○
ROOMY	○	○	○	○	○
T P	○	○	○	○	○
FLUSH	○	○	○	○	○
SPRAY	○	○	○	○	○
OVERALL	○	○	○	○	○

The Dump Files

Please Seat Yourself

Date

___ - ___ - ___

Favorite Song At The Moment

Song _____

Artist _____

Favorite Movie At The Moment

_____

URGENCY

WATCH OUT!
NORMAL
LOW
SHADE

Name

_____

Time In	Time Out
_____ A / P	_____ A / P

What Brings You Here?

#1 _____   #2 _____   #3 _____

Words Of Encouragement

_____

_____

_____

_____

Plans For The Day

_____

_____

_____

_____

Did You Search The Web?

Yes ○   No ○

If So, For... _____

_____

Your Favorite Name For This Room

Bathroom	○	The Crapper	○
The Throne	○	The Shitter	○
The Can	○	The Pot	○
Powder Room	○	The Loo	○
The Jon	○	Other: _____	

ROOM RATINGS:

	1	2	3	4	5
CLEAN	○	○	○	○	○
COMFORTABLE	○	○	○	○	○
READING MATERIALS	○	○	○	○	○
ROOMY	○	○	○	○	○
T P	○	○	○	○	○
FLUSH	○	○	○	○	○
SPRAY	○	○	○	○	○
OVERALL	○	○	○	○	○

The Dump Files

Please Seat Yourself

Date

___-___-___

Name

_____

Favorite Song At The Moment

Song _____

Artist _____

Time In   Time Out

_____ A / P   _____ A / P

What Brings You Here?

#1_____   #2_____   #3_____

Your Favorite Name For This Room

Bathroom	○	The Crapper	○
The Throne	○	The Shitter	○
The Can	○	The Pot	○
Powder Room	○	The Loo	○
The Jon	○	Other: _____	

Favorite Movie At The Moment

_____

Words Of Encouragement

_____

_____

_____

_____

URGENCY

WATCH OUT!
NORMAL
LOW
SHADE

Plans For The Day

_____

_____

_____

ROOM RATINGS:

	1	2	3	4	5
CLEAN	○	○	○	○	○
COMFORTABLE	○	○	○	○	○
READING MATERIALS	○	○	○	○	○
ROOMY	○	○	○	○	○
T P	○	○	○	○	○
FLUSH	○	○	○	○	○
SPRAY	○	○	○	○	○
OVERALL	○	○	○	○	○

The Dump Files

Please Seat Yourself

Date

- - - _____

Favorite Song At The Moment

Song _____

Artist _____

Favorite Movie At The Moment

_____

URGENCY

| WATCH OUT! |
| NORMAL |
| LOW |
| SHADE |

Name

_____

Time In   Time Out

_____ A / P   _____ A / P

What Brings You Here?

#1 _____   #2 _____   #3 _____

Words Of Encouragement

_____
_____
_____
_____

Plans For The Day

_____
_____
_____

Did You Search The Web?

Yes ○   No ○

If So, For... _____
_____

Your Favorite Name For This Room

Bathroom	○	The Crapper	○
The Throne	○	The Shitter	○
The Can	○	The Pot	○
Powder Room	○	The Loo	○
The Jon	○	Other: _____	

ROOM RATINGS:

	1	2	3	4	5
CLEAN	○	○	○	○	○
COMFORTABLE	○	○	○	○	○
READING MATERIALS	○	○	○	○	○
ROOMY	○	○	○	○	○
T P	○	○	○	○	○
FLUSH	○	○	○	○	○
SPRAY	○	○	○	○	○
OVERALL	○	○	○	○	○

The Dump Files

Please Seat Yourself

Date
___ - ___ - ___
_____

Favorite Song At The Moment
Song _____

Artist _____

Favorite Movie At The Moment
_____

URGENCY

WATCH OUT!
NORMAL
LOW
SHADE

Name
_____

Time In _____ A / P

Time Out _____ A / P

What Brings You Here?
#1 _____ #2 _____ #3 _____

Words Of Encouragement
_____
_____
_____
_____

Plans For The Day
_____
_____
_____

Did You Search The Web?
Yes ○   No ○

If So, For... _____
_____

Your Favorite Name For This Room

Bathroom	○	The Crapper	○
The Throne	○	The Shitter	○
The Can	○	The Pot	○
Powder Room	○	The Loo	○
The Jon	○	Other: _____	

ROOM RATINGS:

	1	2	3	4	5
CLEAN	○	○	○	○	○
COMFORTABLE	○	○	○	○	○
READING MATERIALS	○	○	○	○	○
ROOMY	○	○	○	○	○
T P	○	○	○	○	○
FLUSH	○	○	○	○	○
SPRAY	○	○	○	○	○
OVERALL	○	○	○	○	○

The Dump Files

Please Seat Yourself

Date

_ _ _

_____

Favorite Song At The Moment

Song _____

Artist _____

Favorite Movie At The Moment

_____

URGENCY

WATCH OUT!
NORMAL
LOW
SHADE

Name

_____

Time In	Time Out
_____ A / P	_____ A / P

What Brings You Here?

#1 _____   #2 _____   #3 _____

Words Of Encouragement

_____
_____
_____
_____

Plans For The Day

_____
_____
_____
_____

Did You Search The Web?

Yes ○   No ○

If So, For... _____
_____

Your Favorite Name For This Room

Bathroom	○	The Crapper	○
The Throne	○	The Shitter	○
The Can	○	The Pot	○
Powder Room	○	The Loo	○
The Jon	○	Other: _____	

ROOM RATINGS:

	1	2	3	4	5
CLEAN	○	○	○	○	○
COMFORTABLE	○	○	○	○	○
READING MATERIALS	○	○	○	○	○
ROOMY	○	○	○	○	○
T P	○	○	○	○	○
FLUSH	○	○	○	○	○
SPRAY	○	○	○	○	○
OVERALL	○	○	○	○	○

The Dump Files

Please Seat Yourself

Date
___ - ___ - ___

Name
_____

Did You Search The Web?
Yes ○   No ○

If So, For... _____
_____

Favorite Song At The Moment

Song _____

Artist _____

Time In   Time Out
_____ A / P   _____ A / P

What Brings You Here?

#1 _____   #2 _____   #3 _____

Your Favorite Name For This Room

Bathroom	○	The Crapper	○
The Throne	○	The Shitter	○
The Can	○	The Pot	○
Powder Room	○	The Loo	○
The Jon	○	Other: _____	

Favorite Movie At The Moment
_____

Words Of Encouragement
_____
_____
_____
_____

ROOM RATINGS:

	1	2	3	4	5
CLEAN	○	○	○	○	○
COMFORTABLE	○	○	○	○	○
READING MATERIALS	○	○	○	○	○
ROOMY	○	○	○	○	○
T P	○	○	○	○	○
FLUSH	○	○	○	○	○
SPRAY	○	○	○	○	○
OVERALL	○	○	○	○	○

URGENCY

WATCH OUT!
NORMAL
LOW
SHADE

Plans For The Day
_____
_____
_____

The Dump Files

Please Seat Yourself

Date

_____ - _____ - _____

Name

_____

Did You Search The Web?

Yes ○   No ○

If So, For... _____

_____

Favorite Song At The Moment

Song _____

Artist _____

Time In   Time Out

_____ A / P   _____ A / P

What Brings You Here?

#1 _____   #2 _____   #3 _____

Your Favorite Name For This Room

Bathroom	○	The Crapper	○
The Throne	○	The Shitter	○
The Can	○	The Pot	○
Powder Room	○	The Loo	○
The Jon	○	Other: _____	

Favorite Movie At The Moment

_____

Words Of Encouragement

_____

_____

_____

_____

URGENCY

WATCH OUT!
NORMAL
LOW
SHADE

Plans For The Day

_____

_____

_____

_____

ROOM RATINGS:

	1	2	3	4	5
CLEAN	○	○	○	○	○
COMFORTABLE	○	○	○	○	○
READING MATERIALS	○	○	○	○	○
ROOMY	○	○	○	○	○
T P	○	○	○	○	○
FLUSH	○	○	○	○	○
SPRAY	○	○	○	○	○
OVERALL	○	○	○	○	○

The Dumb Files

Please Seat Yourself

Date

_____ - _____ - _____

Name

_____

Did You Search The Web?

Yes ○   No ○

If So, For... _____

_____

Favorite Song At The Moment

Song   _____

Artist   _____

Time In   Time Out

_____ A / P   _____ A / P

What Brings You Here?

#1 _____   #2 _____   #3 _____

Your Favorite Name For This Room

Bathroom	○	The Crapper	○
The Throne	○	The Shitter	○
The Can	○	The Pot	○
Powder Room	○	The Loo	○
The Jon	○	Other: _____	

Favorite Movie At The Moment

_____

Words Of Encouragement

_____

_____

_____

_____

URGENCY

WATCH OUT!
NORMAL
LOW
SHADE

Plans For The Day

_____

_____

_____

ROOM RATINGS:

	1	2	3	4	5
CLEAN	○	○	○	○	○
COMFORTABLE	○	○	○	○	○
READING MATERIALS	○	○	○	○	○
ROOMY	○	○	○	○	○
T P	○	○	○	○	○
FLUSH	○	○	○	○	○
SPRAY	○	○	○	○	○
OVERALL	○	○	○	○	○

The Dump Files

Please Seat Yourself

Date

_ - _ - _____

Favorite Song At The Moment

Song _____

Artist _____

Favorite Movie At The Moment

_____

URGENCY

| WATCH OUT! |
| NORMAL |
| LOW |
| SHADE |

Name

_____

Time In

_____ A / P

Time Out

_____ A / P

What Brings You Here?

#1 _____   #2 _____   #3 _____

Words Of Encouragement

_____

_____

_____

_____

Plans For The Day

_____

_____

_____

Did You Search The Web?

Yes ○   No ○

If So, For... _____

_____

Your Favorite Name For This Room

Bathroom	○	The Crapper	○
The Throne	○	The Shitter	○
The Can	○	The Pot	○
Powder Room	○	The Loo	○
The Jon	○	Other: _____

ROOM RATINGS:

	1	2	3	4	5
CLEAN	○	○	○	○	○
COMFORTABLE	○	○	○	○	○
READING MATERIALS	○	○	○	○	○
ROOMY	○	○	○	○	○
T P	○	○	○	○	○
FLUSH	○	○	○	○	○
SPRAY	○	○	○	○	○
OVERALL	○	○	○	○	○

The Dump Files

Please Seat Yourself

Date
_____ - _____ - _____

Name
_____

Did You Search The Web?
Yes ○   No ○

If So, For... _____

_____

Favorite Song At The Moment

Song _____

Artist _____

Time In   Time Out
_____ A / P   _____ A / P

What Brings You Here?
#1 _____   #2 _____   #3 _____

Your Favorite Name For This Room

Bathroom	○	The Crapper	○
The Throne	○	The Shitter	○
The Can	○	The Pot	○
Powder Room	○	The Loo	○
The Jon	○	Other: _____	

Favorite Movie At The Moment

_____

Words Of Encouragement

_____

_____

_____

_____

URGENCY

WATCH OUT!
NORMAL
LOW
SHADE

Plans For The Day

_____

_____

_____

_____

ROOM RATINGS:

	1	2	3	4	5
CLEAN	○	○	○	○	○
COMFORTABLE	○	○	○	○	○
READING MATERIALS	○	○	○	○	○
ROOMY	○	○	○	○	○
T P	○	○	○	○	○
FLUSH	○	○	○	○	○
SPRAY	○	○	○	○	○
OVERALL	○	○	○	○	○

The Dump Files

Please Seat Yourself

Date

- _____ - _____ - _____

Name

_____

Did You Search The Web?

Yes ○   No ○

If So, For... _____

_____

Favorite Song At The Moment

Song _____

Artist _____

Time In   Time Out

_____ A / P   _____ A / P

Your Favorite Name For This Room

Bathroom	○	The Crapper	○
The Throne	○	The Shitter	○
The Can	○	The Pot	○
Powder Room	○	The Loo	○
The Jon	○	Other: _____	

What Brings You Here?

#1 _____   #2 _____   #3 _____

Favorite Movie At The Moment

_____

Words Of Encouragement

_____

_____

_____

_____

URGENCY

WATCH OUT!
NORMAL
LOW
SHADE

ROOM RATINGS:

	1	2	3	4	5
CLEAN	○	○	○	○	○
COMFORTABLE	○	○	○	○	○
READING MATERIALS	○	○	○	○	○
ROOMY	○	○	○	○	○
T P	○	○	○	○	○
FLUSH	○	○	○	○	○
SPRAY	○	○	○	○	○
OVERALL	○	○	○	○	○

Plans For The Day

_____

_____

_____

The Dump Files

Please Seat Yourself

Date
___ - ___ - ___

Favorite Song At The Moment

Song _____

Artist _____

Favorite Movie At The Moment

_____

URGENCY

| WATCH OUT! |
| NORMAL |
| LOW |
| SHADE |

Name
_____

| Time In | Time Out |
| _____ A / P | _____ A / P |

What Brings You Here?

#1 _____ #2 _____ #3 _____

Words Of Encouragement

_____

_____

_____

_____

Plans For The Day

_____

_____

_____

Did You Search The Web?

Yes ○   No ○

If So, For... _____

_____

Your Favorite Name For This Room

Bathroom ○	The Crapper ○
The Throne ○	The Shitter ○
The Can ○	The Pot ○
Powder Room ○	The Loo ○
The Jon ○	Other: _____

ROOM RATINGS:

	1	2	3	4	5
CLEAN	○	○	○	○	○
COMFORTABLE	○	○	○	○	○
READING MATERIALS	○	○	○	○	○
ROOMY	○	○	○	○	○
T P	○	○	○	○	○
FLUSH	○	○	○	○	○
SPRAY	○	○	○	○	○
OVERALL	○	○	○	○	○

The Dump Files
Please Seat Yourself

Date
- - -
_____

Name
_____

Favorite Song At The Moment

Song _____

Artist _____

Time In   Time Out
_____ A / P   _____ A / P

Your Favorite Name For This Room

Bathroom	○	The Crapper	○
The Throne	○	The Shitter	○
The Can	○	The Pot	○
Powder Room	○	The Loo	○
The Jon	○	Other: _____	

What Brings You Here?

#1 _____ #2 _____ #3 _____

Favorite Movie At The Moment

_____

Words Of Encouragement

_____
_____
_____
_____
_____

ROOM RATINGS:

	1	2	3	4	5
CLEAN	○	○	○	○	○
COMFORTABLE	○	○	○	○	○
READING MATERIALS	○	○	○	○	○
ROOMY	○	○	○	○	○
T P	○	○	○	○	○
FLUSH	○	○	○	○	○
SPRAY	○	○	○	○	○
OVERALL	○	○	○	○	○

URGENCY

WATCH OUT!
NORMAL
LOW
SHADE

Plans For The Day

_____
_____
_____
_____

The Dump Files

Please Seat Yourself

Date
_____ - _____ - _____

Name
_____

Did You Search The Web?
Yes ○   No ○

If So, For... _____

_____

Favorite Song At The Moment
Song _____

Artist _____

Time In   Time Out
_____ A / P   _____ A / P

What Brings You Here?
#1 _____ #2 _____ #3 _____

Your Favorite Name For This Room
Bathroom ○   The Crapper ○
The Throne ○   The Shitter ○
The Can ○   The Pot ○
Powder Room ○   The Loo ○
The Jon ○   Other: _____

Favorite Movie At The Moment
_____

Words Of Encouragement
_____
_____
_____
_____

ROOM RATINGS:
	1	2	3	4	5
CLEAN	○	○	○	○	○
COMFORTABLE	○	○	○	○	○
READING MATERIALS	○	○	○	○	○
ROOMY	○	○	○	○	○
T P	○	○	○	○	○
FLUSH	○	○	○	○	○
SPRAY	○	○	○	○	○
OVERALL	○	○	○	○	○

URGENCY
WATCH OUT!
NORMAL
LOW
SHADE

Plans For The Day
_____
_____
_____
_____

The Dump Files
Please Seat Yourself

Date
- - -
_____

Favorite Song At The Moment
Song _____
Artist _____

Favorite Movie At The Moment
_____

URGENCY

| WATCH OUT! |
| NORMAL |
| LOW |
| SHADE |

Name
_____

Time In   Time Out
_____ A / P   _____ A / P

What Brings You Here?
#1 _____   #2 _____   #3 _____

Words Of Encouragement
_____
_____
_____
_____

Plans For The Day
_____
_____
_____

Did You Search The Web?
Yes ○   No ○
If So, For... _____
_____

Your Favorite Name For This Room
Bathroom   ○   The Crapper   ○
The Throne   ○   The Shitter   ○
The Can   ○   The Pot   ○
Powder Room   ○   The Loo   ○
The Jon   ○   Other: _____

ROOM RATINGS:

	1	2	3	4	5
CLEAN	○	○	○	○	○
COMFORTABLE	○	○	○	○	○
READING MATERIALS	○	○	○	○	○
ROOMY	○	○	○	○	○
T P	○	○	○	○	○
FLUSH	○	○	○	○	○
SPRAY	○	○	○	○	○
OVERALL	○	○	○	○	○

The Dump Files

Please Seat Yourself

Date

___ - ___ - ___

Name

_____

Did You Search The Web?

Yes ○   No ○

If So, For... _____

_____

Favorite Song At The Moment

Song _____

Artist _____

Time In   Time Out

_____ A / P   _____ A / P

What Brings You Here?

#1_____ #2_____ #3_____

Your Favorite Name For This Room

Bathroom	○	The Crapper	○
The Throne	○	The Shitter	○
The Can	○	The Pot	○
Powder Room	○	The Loo	○
The Jon	○	Other: _____	

Favorite Movie At The Moment

_____

Words Of Encouragement

_____

_____

_____

_____

URGENCY

WATCH OUT!
NORMAL
LOW
SHADE

Plans For The Day

_____

_____

_____

ROOM RATINGS:

	1	2	3	4	5
CLEAN	○	○	○	○	○
COMFORTABLE	○	○	○	○	○
READING MATERIALS	○	○	○	○	○
ROOMY	○	○	○	○	○
T P	○	○	○	○	○
FLUSH	○	○	○	○	○
SPRAY	○	○	○	○	○
OVERALL	○	○	○	○	○

The Dump Files

Please Seat Yourself

Date

_ _ _ _ _

Name

_____

Did You Search The Web?

Yes ○   No ○

If So, For... _____

_____

Favorite Song At The Moment

Song _____

Artist _____

Time In   Time Out

_____ A / P   _____ A / P

What Brings You Here?

#1 _____   #2 _____   #3 _____

Your Favorite Name For This Room

Bathroom	○	The Crapper	○
The Throne	○	The Shitter	○
The Can	○	The Pot	○
Powder Room	○	The Loo	○
The Jon	○	Other: _____	

Favorite Movie At The Moment

_____

Words Of Encouragement

_____

_____

_____

_____

URGENCY

WATCH OUT!
NORMAL
LOW
SHADE

Plans For The Day

_____

_____

_____

ROOM RATINGS:

	1	2	3	4	5
CLEAN	○	○	○	○	○
COMFORTABLE	○	○	○	○	○
READING MATERIALS	○	○	○	○	○
ROOMY	○	○	○	○	○
T P	○	○	○	○	○
FLUSH	○	○	○	○	○
SPRAY	○	○	○	○	○
OVERALL	○	○	○	○	○

The Dump Files

Please Seat Yourself

Date

____ - ____ - ____

Name

_____

Did You Search The Web?

Yes ○   No ○

If So, For... _____

_____

Favorite Song At The Moment

Song _____

Artist _____

Time In   Time Out

_____ A / P   _____ A / P

What Brings You Here?

#1 _____ #2 _____ #3 _____

Your Favorite Name For This Room

Bathroom	○	The Crapper	○
The Throne	○	The Shitter	○
The Can	○	The Pot	○
Powder Room	○	The Loo	○
The Jon	○	Other: _____	

Favorite Movie At The Moment

_____

Words Of Encouragement

_____

_____

_____

_____

ROOM RATINGS:

	1	2	3	4	5
CLEAN	○	○	○	○	○
COMFORTABLE	○	○	○	○	○
READING MATERIALS	○	○	○	○	○
ROOMY	○	○	○	○	○
T P	○	○	○	○	○
FLUSH	○	○	○	○	○
SPRAY	○	○	○	○	○
OVERALL	○	○	○	○	○

URGENCY

WATCH OUT!
NORMAL
LOW
SHADE

Plans For The Day

_____

_____

_____

_____

The Dump Files
Please Seat Yourself

Date
_ - _
_____

Name
_____

Did You Search The Web?
Yes ○   No ○

If So, For... _____
_____

Favorite Song At The Moment
Song _____

Artist _____

Time In   Time Out
_____ A / P   _____ A / P

What Brings You Here?
#1 _____ #2 _____ #3 _____

Your Favorite Name For This Room
Bathroom ○   The Crapper ○
The Throne ○   The Shitter ○
The Can ○   The Pot ○
Powder Room ○   The Loo ○
The Jon ○   Other: _____

Favorite Movie At The Moment
_____

Words Of Encouragement
_____
_____
_____
_____
_____

URGENCY

| WATCH OUT! |
| NORMAL |
| LOW |
| SHADE |

Plans For The Day
_____
_____
_____
_____

ROOM RATINGS:

	1	2	3	4	5
CLEAN	○	○	○	○	○
COMFORTABLE	○	○	○	○	○
READING MATERIALS	○	○	○	○	○
ROOMY	○	○	○	○	○
T P	○	○	○	○	○
FLUSH	○	○	○	○	○
SPRAY	○	○	○	○	○
OVERALL	○	○	○	○	○

The Dump Files

Please Seat Yourself

Date
___ - ___ - ___

Name
_____

Did You Search The Web?
Yes ○   No ○

If So, For... _____
_____

Favorite Song At The Moment
Song _____
Artist _____

Time In   Time Out
_____ A / P   _____ A / P

Your Favorite Name For This Room
Bathroom ○   The Crapper ○
The Throne ○   The Shitter ○
The Can ○   The Pot ○
Powder Room ○   The Loo ○
The Jon ○   Other: _____

What Brings You Here?
#1 _____   #2 _____   #3 _____

Favorite Movie At The Moment
_____

Words Of Encouragement
_____
_____
_____
_____

URGENCY

| WATCH OUT! |
| NORMAL |
| LOW |
| SHADE |

Plans For The Day
_____
_____
_____

ROOM RATINGS:

	1	2	3	4	5
CLEAN	○	○	○	○	○
COMFORTABLE	○	○	○	○	○
READING MATERIALS	○	○	○	○	○
ROOMY	○	○	○	○	○
T P	○	○	○	○	○
FLUSH	○	○	○	○	○
SPRAY	○	○	○	○	○
OVERALL	○	○	○	○	○

The Dump Files

Please Seat Yourself

Date

___ - ___ - ___

Favorite Song At The Moment

Song _____

Artist _____

Favorite Movie At The Moment

_____

URGENCY

WATCH OUT!
NORMAL
LOW
SHADE

Name

_____

Time In	Time Out
_____ A / P	_____ A / P

What Brings You Here?

#1 _____ #2 _____ #3 _____

Words Of Encouragement

_____
_____
_____
_____

Plans For The Day

_____
_____
_____

Did You Search The Web?

Yes ○   No ○

If So, For... _____
_____

Your Favorite Name For This Room

Bathroom	○	The Crapper	○
The Throne	○	The Shitter	○
The Can	○	The Pot	○
Powder Room	○	The Loo	○
The Jon	○	Other: _____	

ROOM RATINGS:

	1	2	3	4	5
CLEAN	○	○	○	○	○
COMFORTABLE	○	○	○	○	○
READING MATERIALS	○	○	○	○	○
ROOMY	○	○	○	○	○
T P	○	○	○	○	○
FLUSH	○	○	○	○	○
SPRAY	○	○	○	○	○
OVERALL	○	○	○	○	○

The Dump Files

Please Seat Yourself

Date
___ - ___ - _____

Name
_____

Did You Search The Web?
Yes ○   No ○

If So, For... _____
_____

Favorite Song At The Moment
Song _____

Artist _____

Time In
_____ A / P

Time Out
_____ A / P

What Brings You Here?
#1 _____ #2 _____ #3 _____

Your Favorite Name For This Room
Bathroom	○	The Crapper	○
The Throne	○	The Shitter	○
The Can	○	The Pot	○
Powder Room	○	The Loo	○
The Jon	○	Other: _____	

Favorite Movie At The Moment
_____

Words Of Encouragement
_____
_____
_____
_____

URGENCY

WATCH OUT!
NORMAL
LOW
SHADE

Plans For The Day
_____
_____
_____
_____

ROOM RATINGS:

	1	2	3	4	5
CLEAN	○	○	○	○	○
COMFORTABLE	○	○	○	○	○
READING MATERIALS	○	○	○	○	○
ROOMY	○	○	○	○	○
T P	○	○	○	○	○
FLUSH	○	○	○	○	○
SPRAY	○	○	○	○	○
OVERALL	○	○	○	○	○

The Dump Files

Please Seat Yourself

Date

\- \-
_____

Favorite Song At The Moment

Song _____

Artist _____

Favorite Movie At The Moment

_____

URGENCY

| WATCH OUT! |
| NORMAL |
| LOW |
| SHADE |

Name

_____

Time In   Time Out

_____ A / P   _____ A / P

What Brings You Here?

#1 _____ #2 _____ #3 _____

Words Of Encouragement

_____
_____
_____
_____

Plans For The Day

_____
_____
_____

Did You Search The Web?

Yes ○   No ○

If So, For... _____
_____

Your Favorite Name For This Room

Bathroom	○	The Crapper	○
The Throne	○	The Shitter	○
The Can	○	The Pot	○
Powder Room	○	The Loo	○
The Jon	○	Other: _____	

ROOM RATINGS:

	1	2	3	4	5
CLEAN	○	○	○	○	○
COMFORTABLE	○	○	○	○	○
READING MATERIALS	○	○	○	○	○
ROOMY	○	○	○	○	○
T P	○	○	○	○	○
FLUSH	○	○	○	○	○
SPRAY	○	○	○	○	○
OVERALL	○	○	○	○	○

The Dump Files

Please Seat Yourself

Date	
____ - ____ - ____	

Name

_____

Did You Search The Web?

Yes ○   No ○

If So, For... _____

_____

Favorite Song At The Moment

Song _____

Artist _____

Time In   **Time Out**

_____ A / P   _____ A / P

Your Favorite Name For This Room

Bathroom	○	The Crapper	○
The Throne	○	The Shitter	○
The Can	○	The Pot	○
Powder Room	○	The Loo	○
The Jon	○	Other: _____	

What Brings You Here?

#1 _____   #2 _____   #3 _____

Favorite Movie At The Moment

_____

Words Of Encouragement

_____

_____

_____

_____

ROOM RATINGS:

	1	2	3	4	5
CLEAN	○	○	○	○	○
COMFORTABLE	○	○	○	○	○
READING MATERIALS	○	○	○	○	○
ROOMY	○	○	○	○	○
T P	○	○	○	○	○
FLUSH	○	○	○	○	○
SPRAY	○	○	○	○	○
OVERALL	○	○	○	○	○

URGENCY

WATCH OUT!
NORMAL
LOW
SHADE

Plans For The Day

_____

_____

_____

The Dump Files

Please Seat Yourself

Date

\- \-
_____

Favorite Song
At The Moment

Song _____

Artist _____

Favorite Movie
At The Moment

_____

URGENCY

WATCH OUT!
NORMAL
LOW
SHADE

Name

_____

Time In	Time Out
_____ A / P	_____ A / P

What Brings You Here?

#1 _____   #2 _____   #3 _____

Words Of Encouragement

_____

_____

_____

_____

Plans For The Day

_____

_____

_____

Did You Search The Web?

Yes ○   No ○

If So, For... _____

_____

Your Favorite Name For This Room

Bathroom	○	The Crapper	○
The Throne	○	The Shitter	○
The Can	○	The Pot	○
Powder Room	○	The Loo	○
The Jon	○	Other: _____	

ROOM RATINGS:

	1	2	3	4	5
CLEAN	○	○	○	○	○
COMFORTABLE	○	○	○	○	○
READING MATERIALS	○	○	○	○	○
ROOMY	○	○	○	○	○
T P	○	○	○	○	○
FLUSH	○	○	○	○	○
SPRAY	○	○	○	○	○
OVERALL	○	○	○	○	○

The Dump Files

Please Seat Yourself

Date

___ - ___ - ___

_____

Favorite Song At The Moment

Song _____

Artist _____

Favorite Movie At The Moment

_____

URGENCY

WATCH OUT!
NORMAL
LOW
SHADE

Name

_____

Time In   Time Out

_____ A / P   _____ A / P

What Brings You Here?

#1 _____   #2 _____   #3 _____

Words Of Encouragement

_____
_____
_____
_____

Plans For The Day

_____
_____
_____

Did You Search The Web?

Yes ○   No ○

If So, For... _____

_____

Your Favorite Name For This Room

Bathroom	○	The Crapper	○
The Throne	○	The Shitter	○
The Can	○	The Pot	○
Powder Room	○	The Loo	○
The Jon	○	Other: _____	

ROOM RATINGS:

	1	2	3	4	5
CLEAN	○	○	○	○	○
COMFORTABLE	○	○	○	○	○
READING MATERIALS	○	○	○	○	○
ROOMY	○	○	○	○	○
T P	○	○	○	○	○
FLUSH	○	○	○	○	○
SPRAY	○	○	○	○	○
OVERALL	○	○	○	○	○

The Dump Files

👤 👩

Please Seat Yourself

Date

- - -

_____

Favorite Song At The Moment

Song _____

Artist _____

Favorite Movie At The Moment

_____

URGENCY

WATCH OUT!
NORMAL
LOW
SHADE

Name

_____

Time In   Time Out

_____ A / P   _____ A / P

What Brings You Here?

#1 _____ #2 _____ #3 _____

Words Of Encouragement

_____

_____

_____

_____

Plans For The Day

_____

_____

_____

_____

Did You Search The Web?

Yes ○   No ○

If So, For... _____

_____

Your Favorite Name For This Room

Bathroom	○	The Crapper	○
The Throne	○	The Shitter	○
The Can	○	The Pot	○
Powder Room	○	The Loo	○
The Jon	○	Other: _____	

ROOM RATINGS:

	1	2	3	4	5
CLEAN	○	○	○	○	○
COMFORTABLE	○	○	○	○	○
READING MATERIALS	○	○	○	○	○
ROOMY	○	○	○	○	○
T P	○	○	○	○	○
FLUSH	○	○	○	○	○
SPRAY	○	○	○	○	○
OVERALL	○	○	○	○	○

The Dump Files

Please Seat Yourself

Date

___ - ___ - ___

Favorite Song At The Moment

Song _____

Artist _____

Favorite Movie At The Moment

_____

URGENCY

WATCH OUT!
NORMAL
LOW
SHADE

Name

_____

Time In	Time Out
_____ A / P	_____ A / P

What Brings You Here?

#1 _____   #2 _____   #3 _____

Words Of Encouragement

_____

_____

_____

_____

Plans For The Day

_____

_____

_____

Did You Search The Web?

Yes ○   No ○

If So, For... _____

_____

Your Favorite Name For This Room

Bathroom	○	The Crapper	○
The Throne	○	The Shitter	○
The Can	○	The Pot	○
Powder Room	○	The Loo	○
The Jon	○	Other: _____	

ROOM RATINGS:

	1	2	3	4	5
CLEAN	○	○	○	○	○
COMFORTABLE	○	○	○	○	○
READING MATERIALS	○	○	○	○	○
ROOMY	○	○	○	○	○
T P	○	○	○	○	○
FLUSH	○	○	○	○	○
SPRAY	○	○	○	○	○
OVERALL	○	○	○	○	○

The Dump Files

Please Seat Yourself

Date

___ - ___ - ___

Favorite Song At The Moment

Song _____

Artist _____

Favorite Movie At The Moment

_____

URGENCY

WATCH OUT!
NORMAL
LOW
SHADE

Name

_____

Time In _____ A / P   Time Out _____ A / P

What Brings You Here?

#1 _____ #2 _____ #3 _____

Words Of Encouragement

_____

_____

_____

_____

Plans For The Day

_____

_____

_____

Did You Search The Web?

Yes ○   No ○

If So, For... _____

_____

Your Favorite Name For This Room

Bathroom	○	The Crapper	○
The Throne	○	The Shitter	○
The Can	○	The Pot	○
Powder Room	○	The Loo	○
The Jon	○	Other: _____	

ROOM RATINGS:

	1	2	3	4	5
CLEAN	○	○	○	○	○
COMFORTABLE	○	○	○	○	○
READING MATERIALS	○	○	○	○	○
ROOMY	○	○	○	○	○
T P	○	○	○	○	○
FLUSH	○	○	○	○	○
SPRAY	○	○	○	○	○
OVERALL	○	○	○	○	○

The Dump Files

Please Seat Yourself

Date
_____ - _____ - _____

Name
_____

Did You Search The Web?
Yes ○   No ○

If So, For... _____
_____

Favorite Song At The Moment
Song _____

Artist _____

Time In   Time Out
_____ A / P   _____ A / P

What Brings You Here?
#1 _____   #2 _____   #3 _____

Your Favorite Name For This Room
Bathroom	○	The Crapper	○
The Throne	○	The Shitter	○
The Can	○	The Pot	○
Powder Room	○	The Loo	○
The Jon	○	Other: _____	

Favorite Movie At The Moment
_____

Words Of Encouragement
_____
_____
_____
_____

URGENCY

| WATCH OUT! |
| NORMAL |
| LOW |
| SHADE |

Plans For The Day
_____
_____
_____

ROOM RATINGS:

	1	2	3	4	5
CLEAN	○	○	○	○	○
COMFORTABLE	○	○	○	○	○
READING MATERIALS	○	○	○	○	○
ROOMY	○	○	○	○	○
T P	○	○	○	○	○
FLUSH	○	○	○	○	○
SPRAY	○	○	○	○	○
OVERALL	○	○	○	○	○

The Dump Files

Please Seat Yourself

Date

\- \-

_____

Name

_____

Did You Search The Web?

Yes ○   No ○

If So, For... _____

_____

Favorite Song At The Moment

Song _____

Artist _____

Time In   Time Out

_____ A / P   _____ A / P

What Brings You Here?

#1 _____ #2 _____ #3 _____

Your Favorite Name For This Room

Bathroom	○	The Crapper	○
The Throne	○	The Shitter	○
The Can	○	The Pot	○
Powder Room	○	The Loo	○
The Jon	○	Other: _____	

Favorite Movie At The Moment

_____

Words Of Encouragement

_____

_____

_____

_____

URGENCY

WATCH OUT!
NORMAL
LOW
SHADE

Plans For The Day

_____

_____

_____

_____

ROOM RATINGS:

	1	2	3	4	5
CLEAN	○	○	○	○	○
COMFORTABLE	○	○	○	○	○
READING MATERIALS	○	○	○	○	○
ROOMY	○	○	○	○	○
T P	○	○	○	○	○
FLUSH	○	○	○	○	○
SPRAY	○	○	○	○	○
OVERALL	○	○	○	○	○

The Dump Files

Please Seat Yourself

Date
_____ - _____ - _____

Name
_____

Did You Search The Web?
Yes ○   No ○

If So, For... _____
_____

Favorite Song At The Moment
Song _____

Artist _____

Time In   Time Out
_____ A / P   _____ A / P

What Brings You Here?
#1 _____   #2 _____   #3 _____

Your Favorite Name For This Room

Bathroom	○	The Crapper	○
The Throne	○	The Shitter	○
The Can	○	The Pot	○
Powder Room	○	The Loo	○
The Jon	○	Other: _____	

Favorite Movie At The Moment
_____

Words Of Encouragement
_____
_____
_____
_____

URGENCY

| WATCH OUT! |
| NORMAL |
| LOW |
| SHADE |

Plans For The Day
_____
_____
_____
_____

ROOM RATINGS:

	1	2	3	4	5
CLEAN	○	○	○	○	○
COMFORTABLE	○	○	○	○	○
READING MATERIALS	○	○	○	○	○
ROOMY	○	○	○	○	○
T P	○	○	○	○	○
FLUSH	○	○	○	○	○
SPRAY	○	○	○	○	○
OVERALL	○	○	○	○	○

The Dump Files

Please Seat Yourself

Date

_ - _ - _____

Favorite Song At The Moment

Song _____

Artist _____

Favorite Movie At The Moment

_____

URGENCY

WATCH OUT!
NORMAL
LOW
SHADE

Name

_____

Time In   Time Out

_____ A / P   _____ A / P

What Brings You Here?

#1 _____   #2 _____   #3 _____

Words Of Encouragement

_____
_____
_____
_____

Plans For The Day

_____
_____
_____

Did You Search The Web?

Yes ○   No ○

If So, For... _____
_____

Your Favorite Name For This Room

Bathroom	○	The Crapper	○
The Throne	○	The Shitter	○
The Can	○	The Pot	○
Powder Room	○	The Loo	○
The Jon	○	Other: _____	

ROOM RATINGS:

	1	2	3	4	5
CLEAN	○	○	○	○	○
COMFORTABLE	○	○	○	○	○
READING MATERIALS	○	○	○	○	○
ROOMY	○	○	○	○	○
T P	○	○	○	○	○
FLUSH	○	○	○	○	○
SPRAY	○	○	○	○	○
OVERALL	○	○	○	○	○

The Dump Files

Please Seat Yourself

Date

___ - ___ - ___

Name

_____

Did You Search The Web?

Yes ○   No ○

If So, For... _____

_____

Favorite Song At The Moment

Song _____

Artist _____

Time In   Time Out

_____ A / P   _____ A / P

What Brings You Here?

#1 _____ #2 _____ #3 _____

Your Favorite Name For This Room

Bathroom	○	The Crapper	○
The Throne	○	The Shitter	○
The Can	○	The Pot	○
Powder Room	○	The Loo	○
The Jon	○	Other: _____	

Favorite Movie At The Moment

_____

Words Of Encouragement

_____

_____

_____

_____

URGENCY

WATCH OUT!
NORMAL
LOW
SHADE

Plans For The Day

_____

_____

_____

ROOM RATINGS:

	1	2	3	4	5
CLEAN	○	○	○	○	○
COMFORTABLE	○	○	○	○	○
READING MATERIALS	○	○	○	○	○
ROOMY	○	○	○	○	○
T P	○	○	○	○	○
FLUSH	○	○	○	○	○
SPRAY	○	○	○	○	○
OVERALL	○	○	○	○	○

The Dump Files

Please Seat Yourself

Date

_____ - _____ - _____

Favorite Song At The Moment

Song _____

Artist _____

Favorite Movie At The Moment

_____

URGENCY

| WATCH OUT! |
| NORMAL |
| LOW |
| SHADE |

Name

_____

Time In   Time Out

_____ A / P   _____ A / P

What Brings You Here?

#1 _____   #2 _____   #3 _____

Words Of Encouragement

_____

_____

_____

_____

Plans For The Day

_____

_____

_____

Did You Search The Web?

Yes ○   No ○

If So, For... _____

_____

Your Favorite Name For This Room

Bathroom	○	The Crapper	○
The Throne	○	The Shitter	○
The Can	○	The Pot	○
Powder Room	○	The Loo	○
The Jon	○	Other: _____	

ROOM RATINGS:

	1	2	3	4	5
CLEAN	○	○	○	○	○
COMFORTABLE	○	○	○	○	○
READING MATERIALS	○	○	○	○	○
ROOMY	○	○	○	○	○
T P	○	○	○	○	○
FLUSH	○	○	○	○	○
SPRAY	○	○	○	○	○
OVERALL	○	○	○	○	○

The Dump Files

Please Seat Yourself

Date
_____ - _____ - _____

Name
_____

Did You Search The Web?
Yes ○   No ○

If So, For... _____
_____

Favorite Song At The Moment

Song _____

Artist _____

Time In   Time Out
_____ A / P   _____ A / P

What Brings You Here?

#1 _____ #2 _____ #3 _____

Your Favorite Name For This Room

Bathroom ○		The Crapper ○
The Throne ○		The Shitter ○
The Can ○		The Pot ○
Powder Room ○		The Loo ○
The Jon ○		Other: _____

Favorite Movie At The Moment
_____

Words Of Encouragement
_____
_____
_____
_____

ROOM RATINGS:

	1	2	3	4	5
CLEAN	○	○	○	○	○
COMFORTABLE	○	○	○	○	○
READING MATERIALS	○	○	○	○	○
ROOMY	○	○	○	○	○
T P	○	○	○	○	○
FLUSH	○	○	○	○	○
SPRAY	○	○	○	○	○
OVERALL	○	○	○	○	○

URGENCY

WATCH OUT!
NORMAL
LOW
SHADE

Plans For The Day
_____
_____
_____
_____

The Dump Files

Please Seat Yourself

Date

- _____ - _____ -

Favorite Song At The Moment

Song _____

Artist _____

Favorite Movie At The Moment

_____

URGENCY

| WATCH OUT! |
| NORMAL |
| LOW |
| SHADE |

Name

_____

Time In   Time Out

_____ A / P   _____ A / P

What Brings You Here?

#1 _____   #2 _____   #3 _____

Words Of Encouragement

_____
_____
_____
_____

Plans For The Day

_____
_____
_____

Did You Search The Web?

Yes ○   No ○

If So, For... _____
_____

Your Favorite Name For This Room

Bathroom	○	The Crapper	○
The Throne	○	The Shitter	○
The Can	○	The Pot	○
Powder Room	○	The Loo	○
The Jon	○	Other: _____	

ROOM RATINGS:

	1	2	3	4	5
CLEAN	○	○	○	○	○
COMFORTABLE	○	○	○	○	○
READING MATERIALS	○	○	○	○	○
ROOMY	○	○	○	○	○
T P	○	○	○	○	○
FLUSH	○	○	○	○	○
SPRAY	○	○	○	○	○
OVERALL	○	○	○	○	○

The Dump Files

Please Seat Yourself

Date

___ - ___ - ___

Favorite Song At The Moment

Song _____

Artist _____

Favorite Movie At The Moment

_____

URGENCY

| WATCH OUT! |
| NORMAL |
| LOW |
| SHADE |

Name

_____

Time In   Time Out

_____ A / P   _____ A / P

What Brings You Here?

#1 _____ #2 _____ #3 _____

Words Of Encouragement

_____
_____
_____
_____

Plans For The Day

_____
_____
_____
_____

Did You Search The Web?

Yes ○   No ○

If So, For... _____
_____

Your Favorite Name For This Room

Bathroom	○	The Crapper	○
The Throne	○	The Shitter	○
The Can	○	The Pot	○
Powder Room	○	The Loo	○
The Jon	○	Other: _____	

ROOM RATINGS:

	1	2	3	4	5
CLEAN	○	○	○	○	○
COMFORTABLE	○	○	○	○	○
READING MATERIALS	○	○	○	○	○
ROOMY	○	○	○	○	○
T P	○	○	○	○	○
FLUSH	○	○	○	○	○
SPRAY	○	○	○	○	○
OVERALL	○	○	○	○	○

The Dump Files

Please Seat Yourself

Date

\- \-

_____

Name

_____

Did You Search The Web?

Yes ○   No ○

If So, For... _____

_____

Favorite Song At The Moment

Song _____

Artist _____

Time In   Time Out

_____ A / P   _____ A / P

What Brings You Here?

#1 _____ #2 _____ #3 _____

Your Favorite Name For This Room

Bathroom	○	The Crapper	○
The Throne	○	The Shitter	○
The Can	○	The Pot	○
Powder Room	○	The Loo	○
The Jon	○	Other: _____	

Favorite Movie At The Moment

_____

Words Of Encouragement

_____

_____

_____

_____

URGENCY

WATCH OUT!
NORMAL
LOW
SHADE

Plans For The Day

_____

_____

_____

ROOM RATINGS:

	1	2	3	4	5
CLEAN	○	○	○	○	○
COMFORTABLE	○	○	○	○	○
READING MATERIALS	○	○	○	○	○
ROOMY	○	○	○	○	○
T P	○	○	○	○	○
FLUSH	○	○	○	○	○
SPRAY	○	○	○	○	○
OVERALL	○	○	○	○	○

The Dump Files

Please Seat Yourself

Date

___ - ___ - ___

Favorite Song At The Moment

Song _____

Artist _____

Favorite Movie At The Moment

_____

URGENCY

| WATCH OUT! |
| NORMAL |
| LOW |
| SHADE |

Name

_____

Time In   Time Out

_____ A / P   _____ A / P

What Brings You Here?

#1 _____   #2 _____   #3 _____

Words Of Encouragement

_____
_____
_____
_____

Plans For The Day

_____
_____
_____
_____

Did You Search The Web?

Yes ○   No ○

If So, For... _____

_____

Your Favorite Name For This Room

Bathroom	○	The Crapper	○
The Throne	○	The Shitter	○
The Can	○	The Pot	○
Powder Room	○	The Loo	○
The Jon	○	Other: _____	

ROOM RATINGS:

	1	2	3	4	5
CLEAN	○	○	○	○	○
COMFORTABLE	○	○	○	○	○
READING MATERIALS	○	○	○	○	○
ROOMY	○	○	○	○	○
T P	○	○	○	○	○
FLUSH	○	○	○	○	○
SPRAY	○	○	○	○	○
OVERALL	○	○	○	○	○

The Dump Files

Please Seat Yourself

Date

- __ - __

Name

_____

Did You Search The Web?

Yes ○   No ○

If So, For... _____

_____

Favorite Song At The Moment

Song   _____

Artist _____

Time In   Time Out

_____ A / P   _____ A / P

What Brings You Here?

#1 _____ #2 _____ #3 _____

Your Favorite Name For This Room

Bathroom   ○   The Crapper   ○
The Throne   ○   The Shitter   ○
The Can   ○   The Pot   ○
Powder Room   ○   The Loo   ○
The Jon   ○   Other: _____

Favorite Movie At The Moment

_____

Words Of Encouragement

_____

_____

_____

_____

ROOM RATINGS:

	1	2	3	4	5
CLEAN	○	○	○	○	○
COMFORTABLE	○	○	○	○	○
READING MATERIALS	○	○	○	○	○
ROOMY	○	○	○	○	○
T P	○	○	○	○	○
FLUSH	○	○	○	○	○
SPRAY	○	○	○	○	○
OVERALL	○	○	○	○	○

URGENCY

WATCH OUT!
NORMAL
LOW
SHADE

Plans For The Day

_____

_____

_____

The Dump Files

Please Seat Yourself

Date
_____ - _____ - _____

Name
_____

Did You Search The Web?
Yes ○   No ○

If So, For... _____
_____

Favorite Song At The Moment

Song _____

Artist _____

Time In
_____ A / P

Time Out
_____ A / P

What Brings You Here?
#1 _____   #2 _____   #3 _____

Your Favorite Name For This Room

Bathroom	○	The Crapper	○
The Throne	○	The Shitter	○
The Can	○	The Pot	○
Powder Room	○	The Loo	○
The Jon	○	Other: _____	

Favorite Movie At The Moment
_____

Words Of Encouragement
_____
_____
_____

URGENCY

WATCH OUT!

NORMAL

LOW

SHADE

Plans For The Day
_____
_____
_____

ROOM RATINGS:

	1	2	3	4	5
CLEAN	○	○	○	○	○
COMFORTABLE	○	○	○	○	○
READING MATERIALS	○	○	○	○	○
ROOMY	○	○	○	○	○
T P	○	○	○	○	○
FLUSH	○	○	○	○	○
SPRAY	○	○	○	○	○
OVERALL	○	○	○	○	○

The Dump Files

Please Seat Yourself

Date

- _____ - _____ - _____

Name

_____

Did You Search The Web?

Yes ○   No ○

If So, For... _____

_____

Favorite Song At The Moment

Song _____

Artist _____

Time In   Time Out

_____ A / P   _____ A / P

What Brings You Here?

#1 _____   #2 _____   #3 _____

Your Favorite Name For This Room

Bathroom	○	The Crapper	○
The Throne	○	The Shitter	○
The Can	○	The Pot	○
Powder Room	○	The Loo	○
The Jon	○	Other: _____	

Favorite Movie At The Moment

_____

Words Of Encouragement

_____

_____

_____

_____

URGENCY

WATCH OUT!
NORMAL
LOW
SHADE

Plans For The Day

_____

_____

_____

ROOM RATINGS:

	1	2	3	4	5
CLEAN	○	○	○	○	○
COMFORTABLE	○	○	○	○	○
READING MATERIALS	○	○	○	○	○
ROOMY	○	○	○	○	○
T P	○	○	○	○	○
FLUSH	○	○	○	○	○
SPRAY	○	○	○	○	○
OVERALL	○	○	○	○	○

The Dump Files

Please Seat Yourself

Date

___ - ___ - ___

Name

_____

Did You Search The Web?

Yes ○   No ○

If So, For... _____
_____

Favorite Song At The Moment

Song _____

Artist _____

Time In   Time Out

_____ A / P   _____ A / P

What Brings You Here?

#1 _____ #2 _____ #3 _____

Your Favorite Name For This Room

Bathroom	○	The Crapper	○
The Throne	○	The Shitter	○
The Can	○	The Pot	○
Powder Room	○	The Loo	○
The Jon	○	Other: _____	

Favorite Movie At The Moment

_____

Words Of Encouragement

_____
_____
_____
_____

ROOM RATINGS:

	1	2	3	4	5
CLEAN	○	○	○	○	○
COMFORTABLE	○	○	○	○	○
READING MATERIALS	○	○	○	○	○
ROOMY	○	○	○	○	○
T P	○	○	○	○	○
FLUSH	○	○	○	○	○
SPRAY	○	○	○	○	○
OVERALL	○	○	○	○	○

URGENCY

WATCH OUT!
NORMAL
LOW
SHADE

Plans For The Day

_____
_____
_____

The Dump Files

Please Seat Yourself

Date

- - -

Favorite Song At The Moment

Song _____

Artist _____

Favorite Movie At The Moment

_____

URGENCY

| WATCH OUT! |
| NORMAL |
| LOW |
| SHADE |

Name

_____

Time In   Time Out

_____ A / P   _____ A / P

What Brings You Here?

#1 _____ #2 _____ #3 _____

Words Of Encouragement

_____
_____
_____
_____

Plans For The Day

_____
_____
_____

Did You Search The Web?

Yes ○   No ○

If So, For... _____
_____

Your Favorite Name For This Room

Bathroom	○	The Crapper	○
The Throne	○	The Shitter	○
The Can	○	The Pot	○
Powder Room	○	The Loo	○
The Jon	○	Other: _____	

ROOM RATINGS:

	1	2	3	4	5
CLEAN	○	○	○	○	○
COMFORTABLE	○	○	○	○	○
READING MATERIALS	○	○	○	○	○
ROOMY	○	○	○	○	○
T P	○	○	○	○	○
FLUSH	○	○	○	○	○
SPRAY	○	○	○	○	○
OVERALL	○	○	○	○	○

The Dump Files

Please Seat Yourself

Date

___ - ___ - ___

Favorite Song At The Moment

Song _____

Artist _____

Favorite Movie At The Moment

_____

URGENCY

WATCH OUT!
NORMAL
LOW
SHADE

Name

_____

Time In   Time Out

_____ A / P   _____ A / P

What Brings You Here?

#1 _____ #2 _____ #3 _____

Words Of Encouragement

_____

_____

_____

_____

Plans For The Day

_____

_____

_____

_____

Did You Search The Web?

Yes ○   No ○

If So, For... _____

_____

Your Favorite Name For This Room

Bathroom	○	The Crapper	○
The Throne	○	The Shitter	○
The Can	○	The Pot	○
Powder Room	○	The Loo	○
The Jon	○	Other: _____	

ROOM RATINGS:

	1	2	3	4	5
CLEAN	○	○	○	○	○
COMFORTABLE	○	○	○	○	○
READING MATERIALS	○	○	○	○	○
ROOMY	○	○	○	○	○
T P	○	○	○	○	○
FLUSH	○	○	○	○	○
SPRAY	○	○	○	○	○
OVERALL	○	○	○	○	○

The Dump Files

Please Seat Yourself

Date
- ___ - ___ -

Name
_____

Did You Search The Web?
Yes ○   No ○

If So, For... _____

_____

Favorite Song At The Moment
Song _____
Artist _____

Time In
_____ A / P

Time Out
_____ A / P

What Brings You Here?
#1 _____   #2 _____   #3 _____

Your Favorite Name For This Room
Bathroom ○   The Crapper ○
The Throne ○   The Shitter ○
The Can ○   The Pot ○
Powder Room ○   The Loo ○
The Jon ○   Other: _____

Favorite Movie At The Moment
_____

Words Of Encouragement
_____
_____
_____
_____

URGENCY

WATCH OUT!
NORMAL
LOW
SHADE

Plans For The Day
_____
_____
_____
_____

ROOM RATINGS:

	1	2	3	4	5
CLEAN	○	○	○	○	○
COMFORTABLE	○	○	○	○	○
READING MATERIALS	○	○	○	○	○
ROOMY	○	○	○	○	○
T P	○	○	○	○	○
FLUSH	○	○	○	○	○
SPRAY	○	○	○	○	○
OVERALL	○	○	○	○	○

The Dump Files

Please Seat Yourself

Date

___ - ___ - ___

Favorite Song At The Moment

Song _____

Artist _____

Favorite Movie At The Moment

_____

URGENCY

| WATCH OUT! |
| NORMAL |
| LOW |
| SHADE |

Name

_____

Time In   Time Out

_____ A / P   _____ A / P

What Brings You Here?

#1 _____   #2 _____   #3 _____

Words Of Encouragement

_____

_____

_____

_____

Plans For The Day

_____

_____

_____

Did You Search The Web?

Yes ○   No ○

If So, For... _____

_____

Your Favorite Name For This Room

Bathroom	○	The Crapper	○
The Throne	○	The Shitter	○
The Can	○	The Pot	○
Powder Room	○	The Loo	○
The Jon	○	Other: _____	

ROOM RATINGS:

	1	2	3	4	5
CLEAN	○	○	○	○	○
COMFORTABLE	○	○	○	○	○
READING MATERIALS	○	○	○	○	○
ROOMY	○	○	○	○	○
T P	○	○	○	○	○
FLUSH	○	○	○	○	○
SPRAY	○	○	○	○	○
OVERALL	○	○	○	○	○

The Dump Files

Please Seat Yourself

Date	Name	Did You Search The Web?

Date

____ - ____ - ____

Name

_____

Did You Search The Web?

Yes ○   No ○

If So, For... _____

_____

Favorite Song At The Moment

Song _____

Artist _____

Time In   **Time Out**

_____ A / P   _____ A / P

What Brings You Here?

#1 _____   #2 _____   #3 _____

Your Favorite Name For This Room

Bathroom	○	The Crapper	○
The Throne	○	The Shitter	○
The Can	○	The Pot	○
Powder Room	○	The Loo	○
The Jon	○	Other: _____	

Favorite Movie At The Moment

_____

Words Of Encouragement

_____

_____

_____

_____

URGENCY

WATCH OUT!
NORMAL
LOW
SHADE

Plans For The Day

_____

_____

_____

_____

ROOM RATINGS:

	1	2	3	4	5
CLEAN	○	○	○	○	○
COMFORTABLE	○	○	○	○	○
READING MATERIALS	○	○	○	○	○
ROOMY	○	○	○	○	○
T P	○	○	○	○	○
FLUSH	○	○	○	○	○
SPRAY	○	○	○	○	○
OVERALL	○	○	○	○	○

The Dump Files

Please Seat Yourself

Date

____ - ____ - ____

Favorite Song At The Moment

Song _____

Artist _____

Favorite Movie At The Moment

_____

URGENCY

| WATCH OUT! |
| NORMAL |
| LOW |
| SHADE |

Name

_____

Time In	Time Out
_____ A / P	_____ A / P

What Brings You Here?

#1 _____   #2 _____   #3 _____

Words Of Encouragement

_____
_____
_____
_____

Plans For The Day

_____
_____
_____
_____

Did You Search The Web?

Yes ○   No ○

If So, For... _____
_____

Your Favorite Name For This Room

Bathroom	○	The Crapper	○
The Throne	○	The Shitter	○
The Can	○	The Pot	○
Powder Room	○	The Loo	○
The Jon	○	Other: _____	

ROOM RATINGS:

	1	2	3	4	5
CLEAN	○	○	○	○	○
COMFORTABLE	○	○	○	○	○
READING MATERIALS	○	○	○	○	○
ROOMY	○	○	○	○	○
T P	○	○	○	○	○
FLUSH	○	○	○	○	○
SPRAY	○	○	○	○	○
OVERALL	○	○	○	○	○

The Dump Files

Please Seat Yourself

Date

____ - ____ - ____

Favorite Song At The Moment

Song _____

Artist _____

Favorite Movie At The Moment

_____

URGENCY

| WATCH OUT! |
| NORMAL |
| LOW |
| SHADE |

Name

_____

Time In	Time Out
_____ A / P	_____ A / P

What Brings You Here?

#1 _____ #2 _____ #3 _____

Words Of Encouragement

_____

_____

_____

_____

Plans For The Day

_____

_____

_____

_____

Did You Search The Web?

Yes ○   No ○

If So, For... _____

_____

Your Favorite Name For This Room

Bathroom	○	The Crapper	○
The Throne	○	The Shitter	○
The Can	○	The Pot	○
Powder Room	○	The Loo	○
The Jon	○	Other: ____	

ROOM RATINGS:

	1	2	3	4	5
CLEAN	○	○	○	○	○
COMFORTABLE	○	○	○	○	○
READING MATERIALS	○	○	○	○	○
ROOMY	○	○	○	○	○
T P	○	○	○	○	○
FLUSH	○	○	○	○	○
SPRAY	○	○	○	○	○
OVERALL	○	○	○	○	○

The Dump Files

Please Seat Yourself

Date

_____ - _____ - _____

Name

_____

Favorite Song At The Moment

Song _____

Artist _____

Favorite Movie At The Moment

_____

URGENCY

WATCH OUT!
NORMAL
LOW
SHADE

Time In   Time Out

_____ A / P   _____ A / P

What Brings You Here?

#1 _____   #2 _____   #3 _____

Words Of Encouragement

_____

_____

_____

_____

Plans For The Day

_____

_____

_____

_____

Did You Search The Web?

Yes ○   No ○

If So, For... _____

_____

Your Favorite Name For This Room

Bathroom	○	The Crapper	○
The Throne	○	The Shitter	○
The Can	○	The Pot	○
Powder Room	○	The Loo	○
The Jon	○	Other: _____	

ROOM RATINGS:

	1	2	3	4	5
CLEAN	○	○	○	○	○
COMFORTABLE	○	○	○	○	○
READING MATERIALS	○	○	○	○	○
ROOMY	○	○	○	○	○
T P	○	○	○	○	○
FLUSH	○	○	○	○	○
SPRAY	○	○	○	○	○
OVERALL	○	○	○	○	○

The Dump Files

Please Seat Yourself

Date

_ - _ - _____

Name

_____

Did You Search The Web?

Yes ○   No ○

If So, For... _____

_____

Favorite Song At The Moment

Song _____

Artist _____

Time In   Time Out

_____ A / P   _____ A / P

What Brings You Here?

#1 _____   #2 _____   #3 _____

Your Favorite Name For This Room

Bathroom	○	The Crapper	○
The Throne	○	The Shitter	○
The Can	○	The Pot	○
Powder Room	○	The Loo	○
The Jon	○	Other: _____	

Favorite Movie At The Moment

_____

Words Of Encouragement

_____

_____

_____

_____

URGENCY

WATCH OUT!
NORMAL
LOW
SHADE

Plans For The Day

_____

_____

_____

_____

ROOM RATINGS:

	1	2	3	4	5
CLEAN	○	○	○	○	○
COMFORTABLE	○	○	○	○	○
READING MATERIALS	○	○	○	○	○
ROOMY	○	○	○	○	○
T P	○	○	○	○	○
FLUSH	○	○	○	○	○
SPRAY	○	○	○	○	○
OVERALL	○	○	○	○	○

The Dump Files

Please Seat Yourself

Date

___ - ___ - ___

Name

_____

Did You Search The Web?

Yes ○   No ○

If So, For... _____

_____

Favorite Song At The Moment

Song _____

Artist _____

Time In   Time Out

_____ A / P   _____ A / P

What Brings You Here?

#1 _____ #2 _____ #3 _____

Your Favorite Name For This Room

Bathroom	○	The Crapper	○
The Throne	○	The Shitter	○
The Can	○	The Pot	○
Powder Room	○	The Loo	○
The Jon	○	Other: _____	

Favorite Movie At The Moment

_____

Words Of Encouragement

_____

_____

_____

_____

ROOM RATINGS:

	1	2	3	4	5
CLEAN	○	○	○	○	○
COMFORTABLE	○	○	○	○	○
READING MATERIALS	○	○	○	○	○
ROOMY	○	○	○	○	○
T P	○	○	○	○	○
FLUSH	○	○	○	○	○
SPRAY	○	○	○	○	○
OVERALL	○	○	○	○	○

URGENCY

WATCH OUT!
NORMAL
LOW
SHADE

Plans For The Day

_____

_____

_____

_____

The Dump Files

Please Seat Yourself

Date

_ _

_____

Name

_____

Did You Search The Web?

Yes ○   No ○

If So, For... _____

_____

Favorite Song At The Moment

Song   _____

Artist   _____

Time In   Time Out

_____ A / P   _____ A / P

What Brings You Here?

#1 _____   #2 _____   #3 _____

Your Favorite Name For This Room

Bathroom	○	The Crapper	○
The Throne	○	The Shitter	○
The Can	○	The Pot	○
Powder Room	○	The Loo	○
The Jon	○	Other: _____	

Favorite Movie At The Moment

_____

Words Of Encouragement

_____

_____

_____

_____

ROOM RATINGS:

	1	2	3	4	5
CLEAN	○	○	○	○	○
COMFORTABLE	○	○	○	○	○
READING MATERIALS	○	○	○	○	○
ROOMY	○	○	○	○	○
T P	○	○	○	○	○
FLUSH	○	○	○	○	○
SPRAY	○	○	○	○	○
OVERALL	○	○	○	○	○

URGENCY

WATCH OUT!
NORMAL
LOW
SHADE

Plans For The Day

_____

_____

_____

_____

The Dump Files

Please Seat Yourself

Date

_____ - _____ - _____

Name

_____

Did You Search The Web?

Yes ○   No ○

If So, For... _____

_____

Favorite Song At The Moment

Song _____

Artist _____

Time In   Time Out

_____ A / P   _____ A / P

What Brings You Here?

#1 _____   #2 _____   #3 _____

Your Favorite Name For This Room

Bathroom	○	The Crapper	○
The Throne	○	The Shitter	○
The Can	○	The Pot	○
Powder Room	○	The Loo	○
The Jon	○	Other: _____	

Favorite Movie At The Moment

_____

Words Of Encouragement

_____

_____

_____

_____

URGENCY

WATCH OUT!
NORMAL
LOW
SHADE

Plans For The Day

_____

_____

_____

_____

ROOM RATINGS:

	1	2	3	4	5
CLEAN	○	○	○	○	○
COMFORTABLE	○	○	○	○	○
READING MATERIALS	○	○	○	○	○
ROOMY	○	○	○	○	○
T P	○	○	○	○	○
FLUSH	○	○	○	○	○
SPRAY	○	○	○	○	○
OVERALL	○	○	○	○	○

The Dump Files

Please Seat Yourself

Date

- ــــ - ــــ
_____

Favorite Song At The Moment

Song _____

Artist _____

Favorite Movie At The Moment

_____

URGENCY

WATCH OUT!
NORMAL
LOW
SHADE

Name

_____

Time In   Time Out

_____ A / P   _____ A / P

What Brings You Here?

#1 _____   #2 _____   #3 _____

Words Of Encouragement

_____
_____
_____
_____

Plans For The Day

_____
_____
_____

Did You Search The Web?

Yes ○   No ○

If So, For... _____
_____

Your Favorite Name For This Room

Bathroom	○	The Crapper	○
The Throne	○	The Shitter	○
The Can	○	The Pot	○
Powder Room	○	The Loo	○
The Jon	○	Other: _____	

ROOM RATINGS:

	1	2	3	4	5
CLEAN	○	○	○	○	○
COMFORTABLE	○	○	○	○	○
READING MATERIALS	○	○	○	○	○
ROOMY	○	○	○	○	○
T P	○	○	○	○	○
FLUSH	○	○	○	○	○
SPRAY	○	○	○	○	○
OVERALL	○	○	○	○	○

The Dump Files

Please Seat Yourself

Date

_____ - _____ - _____

Favorite Song At The Moment

Song _____

Artist _____

Favorite Movie At The Moment

_____

URGENCY

WATCH OUT!
NORMAL
LOW
SHADE

Name

_____

Time In   Time Out

_____ A / P   _____ A / P

What Brings You Here?

#1 _____ #2 _____ #3 _____

Words Of Encouragement

_____
_____
_____
_____
_____

Plans For The Day

_____
_____
_____
_____

Did You Search The Web?

Yes ○   No ○

If So, For... _____
_____

Your Favorite Name For This Room

Bathroom	○	The Crapper	○
The Throne	○	The Shitter	○
The Can	○	The Pot	○
Powder Room	○	The Loo	○
The Jon	○	Other: _____	

ROOM RATINGS:

	1	2	3	4	5
CLEAN	○	○	○	○	○
COMFORTABLE	○	○	○	○	○
READING MATERIALS	○	○	○	○	○
ROOMY	○	○	○	○	○
T P	○	○	○	○	○
FLUSH	○	○	○	○	○
SPRAY	○	○	○	○	○
OVERALL	○	○	○	○	○

The Dump Files

Please Seat Yourself

Date
___ - ___ - ___

Name
_____

Did You Search The Web?
Yes ○   No ○

If So, For... _____
_____

Favorite Song At The Moment
Song _____
Artist _____

Time In   Time Out
_____ A / P   _____ A / P

What Brings You Here?
#1 _____ #2 _____ #3 _____

Your Favorite Name For This Room
Bathroom	○	The Crapper	○
The Throne	○	The Shitter	○
The Can	○	The Pot	○
Powder Room	○	The Loo	○
The Jon	○	Other: _____	

Favorite Movie At The Moment
_____

Words Of Encouragement
_____
_____
_____
_____

URGENCY

WATCH OUT!
NORMAL
LOW
SHADE

Plans For The Day
_____
_____
_____

ROOM RATINGS:

	1	2	3	4	5
CLEAN	○	○	○	○	○
COMFORTABLE	○	○	○	○	○
READING MATERIALS	○	○	○	○	○
ROOMY	○	○	○	○	○
T P	○	○	○	○	○
FLUSH	○	○	○	○	○
SPRAY	○	○	○	○	○
OVERALL	○	○	○	○	○

The Dump Files

Please Seat Yourself

Date

___ - ___ - ___

Name

_____

Did You Search The Web?

Yes ○   No ○

If So, For... _____

_____

Favorite Song At The Moment

Song _____

Artist _____

Time In   Time Out

_____ A / P   _____ A / P

What Brings You Here?

#1 _____ #2 _____ #3 _____

Your Favorite Name For This Room

Bathroom ○   The Crapper ○
The Throne ○   The Shitter ○
The Can ○   The Pot ○
Powder Room ○   The Loo ○
The Jon ○   Other: _____

Favorite Movie At The Moment

_____

Words Of Encouragement

_____
_____
_____
_____

URGENCY

| WATCH OUT! |
| NORMAL |
| LOW |
| SHADE |

Plans For The Day

_____
_____
_____
_____

ROOM RATINGS:

	1	2	3	4	5
CLEAN	○	○	○	○	○
COMFORTABLE	○	○	○	○	○
READING MATERIALS	○	○	○	○	○
ROOMY	○	○	○	○	○
T P	○	○	○	○	○
FLUSH	○	○	○	○	○
SPRAY	○	○	○	○	○
OVERALL	○	○	○	○	○

The Dump Files

Please Seat Yourself

Date

_ - _ - _____

Name

_____

Did You Search The Web?

Yes ○   No ○

If So, For... _____
_____

Favorite Song At The Moment

Song _____

Artist _____

Time In   Time Out

_____ A / P   _____ A / P

What Brings You Here?

#1 _____   #2 _____   #3 _____

Your Favorite Name For This Room

Bathroom	○	The Crapper	○
The Throne	○	The Shitter	○
The Can	○	The Pot	○
Powder Room	○	The Loo	○
The Jon	○	Other: _____	

Favorite Movie At The Moment

_____

Words Of Encouragement

_____
_____
_____
_____

URGENCY

WATCH OUT!
NORMAL
LOW
SHADE

Plans For The Day

_____
_____
_____

ROOM RATINGS:

	1	2	3	4	5
CLEAN	○	○	○	○	○
COMFORTABLE	○	○	○	○	○
READING MATERIALS	○	○	○	○	○
ROOMY	○	○	○	○	○
T P	○	○	○	○	○
FLUSH	○	○	○	○	○
SPRAY	○	○	○	○	○
OVERALL	○	○	○	○	○

The Dump Files

Please Seat Yourself

Date
_____ - _____ - _____

Name
_____

Did You Search The Web?
Yes ○   No ○

If So, For... _____
_____

Favorite Song At The Moment
Song _____

Artist _____

Time In   Time Out
_____ A / P   _____ A / P

What Brings You Here?
#1 _____   #2 _____   #3 _____

Your Favorite Name For This Room
Bathroom	○	The Crapper	○
The Throne	○	The Shitter	○
The Can	○	The Pot	○
Powder Room	○	The Loo	○
The Jon	○	Other: _____	

Favorite Movie At The Moment
_____

Words Of Encouragement
_____
_____
_____
_____
_____

URGENCY

WATCH OUT!
NORMAL
LOW
SHADE

Plans For The Day
_____
_____
_____
_____

ROOM RATINGS:

	1	2	3	4	5
CLEAN	○	○	○	○	○
COMFORTABLE	○	○	○	○	○
READING MATERIALS	○	○	○	○	○
ROOMY	○	○	○	○	○
T P	○	○	○	○	○
FLUSH	○	○	○	○	○
SPRAY	○	○	○	○	○
OVERALL	○	○	○	○	○

The Dump Files

Please Seat Yourself

Date

____ - ____ - ____

Name

_____

Did You Search The Web?

Yes ○   No ○

If So, For... _____

_____

Favorite Song At The Moment

Song _____

Artist _____

Time In   Time Out

_____ A / P   _____ A / P

What Brings You Here?

#1 _____   #2 _____   #3 _____

Your Favorite Name For This Room

Bathroom	○	The Crapper	○
The Throne	○	The Shitter	○
The Can	○	The Pot	○
Powder Room	○	The Loo	○
The Jon	○	Other: _____	

Favorite Movie At The Moment

_____

Words Of Encouragement

_____

_____

_____

_____

URGENCY

WATCH OUT!
NORMAL
LOW
SHADE

Plans For The Day

_____

_____

_____

ROOM RATINGS:

	1	2	3	4	5
CLEAN	○	○	○	○	○
COMFORTABLE	○	○	○	○	○
READING MATERIALS	○	○	○	○	○
ROOMY	○	○	○	○	○
T P	○	○	○	○	○
FLUSH	○	○	○	○	○
SPRAY	○	○	○	○	○
OVERALL	○	○	○	○	○

The Dump Files

Please Seat Yourself

Date
_ - _ - _

Name
_____

Did You Search The Web?
Yes ○   No ○

If So, For... _____

_____

Favorite Song At The Moment
Song _____
Artist _____

Time In   Time Out
_____ A / P   _____ A / P

What Brings You Here?
#1 _____ #2 _____ #3 _____

Your Favorite Name For This Room
Bathroom	○	The Crapper	○
The Throne	○	The Shitter	○
The Can	○	The Pot	○
Powder Room	○	The Loo	○
The Jon	○	Other: _____	

Favorite Movie At The Moment
_____

Words Of Encouragement
_____
_____
_____
_____

URGENCY

WATCH OUT!
NORMAL
LOW
SHADE

Plans For The Day
_____
_____
_____
_____

ROOM RATINGS:

	1	2	3	4	5
CLEAN	○	○	○	○	○
COMFORTABLE	○	○	○	○	○
READING MATERIALS	○	○	○	○	○
ROOMY	○	○	○	○	○
T P	○	○	○	○	○
FLUSH	○	○	○	○	○
SPRAY	○	○	○	○	○
OVERALL	○	○	○	○	○

The Dump Files

Please Seat Yourself

Date
___ - ___ - ___

Name
_____

Did You Search The Web?
Yes ○   No ○

If So, For... _____

_____

Favorite Song At The Moment

Song _____

Artist _____

Time In   Time Out
_____ A / P   _____ A / P

What Brings You Here?

#1_____   #2_____   #3_____

Your Favorite Name For This Room

Bathroom	○	The Crapper	○
The Throne	○	The Shitter	○
The Can	○	The Pot	○
Powder Room	○	The Loo	○
The Jon	○	Other: _____	

Favorite Movie At The Moment

_____

Words Of Encouragement

_____
_____
_____
_____

URGENCY

WATCH OUT!
NORMAL
LOW
SHADE

Plans For The Day

_____
_____
_____

ROOM RATINGS:

	1	2	3	4	5
CLEAN	○	○	○	○	○
COMFORTABLE	○	○	○	○	○
READING MATERIALS	○	○	○	○	○
ROOMY	○	○	○	○	○
T P	○	○	○	○	○
FLUSH	○	○	○	○	○
SPRAY	○	○	○	○	○
OVERALL	○	○	○	○	○

The Dump Files

Please Seat Yourself

Date

_____ - _____ - _____

Favorite Song At The Moment

Song _____

Artist _____

Favorite Movie At The Moment

_____

URGENCY

WATCH OUT!
NORMAL
LOW
SHADE

Name

_____

Time In _____ A / P   Time Out _____ A / P

What Brings You Here?

#1 _____   #2 _____   #3 _____

Words Of Encouragement

_____
_____
_____
_____

Plans For The Day

_____
_____
_____
_____

Did You Search The Web?

Yes ○   No ○

If So, For... _____

_____

Your Favorite Name For This Room

Bathroom	○	The Crapper	○
The Throne	○	The Shitter	○
The Can	○	The Pot	○
Powder Room	○	The Loo	○
The Jon	○	Other: _____	

ROOM RATINGS:

	1	2	3	4	5
CLEAN	○	○	○	○	○
COMFORTABLE	○	○	○	○	○
READING MATERIALS	○	○	○	○	○
ROOMY	○	○	○	○	○
T P	○	○	○	○	○
FLUSH	○	○	○	○	○
SPRAY	○	○	○	○	○
OVERALL	○	○	○	○	○

The Dump Files

Please Seat Yourself

Date

- -
_____

Name

_____

Did You Search The Web?

Yes ○   No ○

If So, For... _____
_____

Favorite Song At The Moment

Song _____

Artist _____

Time In   Time Out

_____ A / P   _____ A / P

What Brings You Here?

#1 _____   #2 _____   #3 _____

Your Favorite Name For This Room

Bathroom	○	The Crapper	○
The Throne	○	The Shitter	○
The Can	○	The Pot	○
Powder Room	○	The Loo	○
The Jon	○	Other: _____	

Favorite Movie At The Moment

_____

Words Of Encouragement

_____
_____
_____
_____

URGENCY

WATCH OUT!
NORMAL
LOW
SHADE

Plans For The Day

_____
_____
_____

ROOM RATINGS:

	1	2	3	4	5
CLEAN	○	○	○	○	○
COMFORTABLE	○	○	○	○	○
READING MATERIALS	○	○	○	○	○
ROOMY	○	○	○	○	○
T P	○	○	○	○	○
FLUSH	○	○	○	○	○
SPRAY	○	○	○	○	○
OVERALL	○	○	○	○	○

The Dump Files
Please Seat Yourself

Date
___ - ___ - ___

Name
_____

Favorite Song At The Moment
Song _____

Artist _____

Favorite Movie At The Moment
_____

URGENCY

| WATCH OUT! |
| NORMAL |
| LOW |
| SHADE |

Time In _____ A / P

Time Out _____ A / P

What Brings You Here?
#1_____   #2_____   #3_____

Words Of Encouragement
_____

_____

_____

_____

Plans For The Day
_____

_____

_____

Did You Search The Web?
Yes ○   No ○

If So, For... _____

_____

Your Favorite Name For This Room

Bathroom	○	The Crapper	○
The Throne	○	The Shitter	○
The Can	○	The Pot	○
Powder Room	○	The Loo	○
The Jon	○	Other: _____	

ROOM RATINGS:

	1	2	3	4	5
CLEAN	○	○	○	○	○
COMFORTABLE	○	○	○	○	○
READING MATERIALS	○	○	○	○	○
ROOMY	○	○	○	○	○
T P	○	○	○	○	○
FLUSH	○	○	○	○	○
SPRAY	○	○	○	○	○
OVERALL	○	○	○	○	○

The Dump Files

Please Seat Yourself

Date	Name	Did You Search The Web?
- - _____	_____	Yes ○ No ○ If So, For... _____ _____

Favorite Song At The Moment

Song _____

Artist _____

Favorite Movie At The Moment

_____

URGENCY

WATCH OUT!
NORMAL
LOW
SHADE

Time In _____ A / P   Time Out _____ A / P

What Brings You Here?

#1 _____   #2 _____   #3 _____

Words Of Encouragement

_____
_____
_____
_____

Plans For The Day

_____
_____
_____

Your Favorite Name For This Room

Bathroom	○	The Crapper	○
The Throne	○	The Shitter	○
The Can	○	The Pot	○
Powder Room	○	The Loo	○
The Jon	○	Other: _____	

ROOM RATINGS:

	1	2	3	4	5
CLEAN	○	○	○	○	○
COMFORTABLE	○	○	○	○	○
READING MATERIALS	○	○	○	○	○
ROOMY	○	○	○	○	○
T P	○	○	○	○	○
FLUSH	○	○	○	○	○
SPRAY	○	○	○	○	○
OVERALL	○	○	○	○	○

The Dump Files

Please Seat Yourself

Date

_____ - _____ - _____

Name

_____

Did You Search The Web?

Yes ○   No ○

If So, For... _____

_____

Favorite Song At The Moment

Song _____

Artist _____

Time In   Time Out

_____ A / P   _____ A / P

What Brings You Here?

#1 _____   #2 _____   #3 _____

Your Favorite Name For This Room

Bathroom   ○   The Crapper   ○
The Throne   ○   The Shitter   ○
The Can   ○   The Pot   ○
Powder Room   ○   The Loo   ○
The Jon   ○   Other: _____

Favorite Movie At The Moment

_____

Words Of Encouragement

_____
_____
_____
_____
_____

URGENCY

| WATCH OUT! |
| NORMAL |
| LOW |
| SHADE |

Plans For The Day

_____
_____
_____
_____

ROOM RATINGS:

	1	2	3	4	5
CLEAN	○	○	○	○	○
COMFORTABLE	○	○	○	○	○
READING MATERIALS	○	○	○	○	○
ROOMY	○	○	○	○	○
T P	○	○	○	○	○
FLUSH	○	○	○	○	○
SPRAY	○	○	○	○	○
OVERALL	○	○	○	○	○

The Dump Files

Please Seat Yourself

Date	Name	Did You Search The Web?
- - _____	_____	Yes ○ No ○ If So, For... _____ _____

Favorite Song At The Moment

Song _____

Artist _____

Time In   Time Out
_____ A / P   _____ A / P

What Brings You Here?
#1 _____   #2 _____   #3 _____

Your Favorite Name For This Room

Bathroom	○	The Crapper	○
The Throne	○	The Shitter	○
The Can	○	The Pot	○
Powder Room	○	The Loo	○
The Jon	○	Other: _____	

Favorite Movie At The Moment

_____

Words Of Encouragement

_____

_____

_____

_____

URGENCY

WATCH OUT!
NORMAL
LOW
SHADE

Plans For The Day

_____

_____

_____

ROOM RATINGS:

	1	2	3	4	5
CLEAN	○	○	○	○	○
COMFORTABLE	○	○	○	○	○
READING MATERIALS	○	○	○	○	○
ROOMY	○	○	○	○	○
T P	○	○	○	○	○
FLUSH	○	○	○	○	○
SPRAY	○	○	○	○	○
OVERALL	○	○	○	○	○

The Dump Files

Please Seat Yourself

Date

___ - ___ - ___

Name

_____

Did You Search The Web?

Yes ○   No ○

If So, For... _____

_____

Favorite Song At The Moment

Song _____

Artist _____

Time In   Time Out

_____ A / P   _____ A / P

What Brings You Here?

#1 _____ #2 _____ #3 _____

Your Favorite Name For This Room

Bathroom ○   The Crapper ○
The Throne ○   The Shitter ○
The Can ○   The Pot ○
Powder Room ○   The Loo ○
The Jon ○   Other: _____

Favorite Movie At The Moment

_____

Words Of Encouragement

_____
_____
_____
_____

ROOM RATINGS:

	1	2	3	4	5
CLEAN	○	○	○	○	○
COMFORTABLE	○	○	○	○	○
READING MATERIALS	○	○	○	○	○
ROOMY	○	○	○	○	○
T P	○	○	○	○	○
FLUSH	○	○	○	○	○
SPRAY	○	○	○	○	○
OVERALL	○	○	○	○	○

URGENCY

| WATCH OUT! |
| NORMAL |
| LOW |
| SHADE |

Plans For The Day

_____
_____
_____
_____

The Dump Files

Please Seat Yourself

Date

- -
_____

Favorite Song At The Moment

Song _____

Artist _____

Favorite Movie At The Moment

_____

URGENCY

| WATCH OUT! |
| NORMAL |
| LOW |
| SHADE |

Name

_____

Time In   Time Out

_____ A / P   _____ A / P

What Brings You Here?

#1 _____   #2 _____   #3 _____

Words Of Encouragement

_____
_____
_____
_____
_____

Plans For The Day

_____
_____
_____
_____

Did You Search The Web?

Yes ○   No ○

If So, For... _____
_____

Your Favorite Name For This Room

Bathroom	○	The Crapper	○
The Throne	○	The Shitter	○
The Can	○	The Pot	○
Powder Room	○	The Loo	○
The Jon	○	Other: _____	

ROOM RATINGS:

	1	2	3	4	5
CLEAN	○	○	○	○	○
COMFORTABLE	○	○	○	○	○
READING MATERIALS	○	○	○	○	○
ROOMY	○	○	○	○	○
T P	○	○	○	○	○
FLUSH	○	○	○	○	○
SPRAY	○	○	○	○	○
OVERALL	○	○	○	○	○

THE DUMP FILES

Elements of this book
has been provided by:
Freedesignfile.com
All-free-download.com
Vectorportal.com

www.ingramcontent.com/pod-product-compliance
Lightning Source LLC
Chambersburg PA
CBHW041652260326

41914CB00018B/1622